How to Build a

~~Share Portfolio~~

A practical guide to selecting and
monitoring a portfolio of shares

Rodney Hobson

HARRIMAN HOUSE LTD

3A Penns Road
Petersfield
Hampshire
GU32 2EW
GREAT BRITAIN

Tel: +44 (0)1730 233870
Fax: +44 (0)1730 233880
Email: enquiries@harriman-house.com
Website: www.harriman-house.com

First published in Great Britain in 2011
Copyright © Harriman House Ltd

The right of Rodney Hobson to be identified as Author has been asserted in accordance
with the Copyright, Design and Patents Act 1988.

ISBN: 978-0857190-21-5

British Library Cataloguing in Publication Data
A CIP catalogue record for this book can be obtained from the British Library.

Printed and bound by CPI Antony Rowe, Chippenham and Eastbourne.

Disclaimer

All the many case studies included in this book refer to genuine announcements and events on the London Stock Exchange. However, they represent the situation at each company referred to at a given moment in time. Circumstances change and issues raised at one juncture may be resolved or superseded. Similarly, new challenges arise over time.

Therefore nothing in this book constitutes a recommendation to buy or sell shares in a specific company or sector. The sample portfolio is for illustrative purposes only. Investors must exercise their own judgement.

Readers interested in finding out more about a particular company should read the latest stock market announcements.

At the time of writing the author held shares in Royal Dutch Shell, National Grid and Hornby but not in any other company mentioned in this book. These investments were being held for the long term.

There is also reference to tobacco companies. For the record, the author has never smoked.

About the author

Rodney Hobson is an experienced financial journalist who has held senior editorial positions with publications in the UK and Asia. Among posts he has held are news editor for the business section of *The Times*, editor of *Shares* magazine, business editor of the *Singapore Monitor* and deputy business editor of the *Far Eastern Economic Review*.

He has also contributed to the City pages of the *Daily Mail*, *The Independent* and *The Independent on Sunday*.

Rodney was at the forefront in the setting up of financial websites, firstly as Head of News for the launch of *Citywire* and more recently as Editor of *Hemscott*, for whom he continues to write a weekly investment email. He has been featured on BBC TV and radio and on CNBC, as well as appearing as a guest speaker at conferences such as the World Money Show.

He is the author of *Shares Made Simple*, the authoritative beginner's guide to the stock market, *Small Companies, Big Profits*, a guide to investing in smaller quoted companies, and *Understanding Company News*, the guide to interpreting stock market announcements. All are published by Harriman House.

Rodney is registered as a representative with the Financial Services Authority. He is married with one daughter.

Other books by the same author:

www.harriman-house.com/sharesmadesimple

www.harriman-house.com/smallcompanies

www.harriman-house.com/understandingcompanynews

Rodney Hobson's personal website is **www.rodneyhobson.co.uk**

Contents

Preface   xi

Introduction   xv

Part I – The Choice of Assets   1

Chapter 1. The Range of Assets   3

What is a portfolio?   3

Shares   5

Cash   6

Gold   7

Gilts   10

Company bonds   11

Property   12

Works of art   13

Collectibles   13

Funds   14

Exchange Traded Funds   15

Summary comparison of assets   18

Costs   19

Mix and match   20

Why build a properly constructed portfolio?   21

Lessons learnt   22

Chapter 2. The Attractions of Equities   23

Performance   23

Diversification   26

Foreign stocks   28

Lessons learnt   34

Part II – Building a Portfolio   35

Chapter 3. Basic Decisions   37

Investing for income   37

Investing for growth   38

How many? 39

Pounds, not numbers 41

Sectors 41

Weightings 42

Over and under weight 45

Lessons learnt 46

Chapter 4. Top Down and Bottom Up 47

Top down 47

Bottom up 52

Best of both worlds 57

Chapter 5. Fundamentals 59

What to look for 60

Company analysis 61

Lessons learnt 75

Chapter 6. Choosing Between Cyclicals and Defensives 77

Timing issues 79

Visibility of earnings 81

Cyclicals 82

Defensives 89

Lessons learnt 98

Chapter 7. Investing for Dividends 99

Where to look for dividends 107

Dividend cuts 110

High payers 112

Dividends in dollars 112

Lessons learnt 113

Chapter 8. Investing for Capital Growth 115

Growth companies 116

Value investing 117

Case Study: Dogs of the Dow 118

Lessons learnt 122

Chapter 9. When to Invest   **123**

Bull or bear market   123

Volatile markets   124

Buying opportunities   124

Pound cost averaging   129

Lessons learnt   130

Chapter 10. New Issues   **131**

Taken on merit   133

Pricing   133

Book building   134

Lessons learnt   139

Chapter 11. When Share Prices Fall   141

Catching falling knives   147

Profit warnings   149

Lessons learnt   151

Part III – Managing Your Portfolio   **153**

Chapter 12. Monitoring Your Portfolio   **155**

How often to monitor   157

Measuring performance   158

Benefits of monitoring   162

Chapter 13. Stop Losses and Averaging Down   **165**

Stop losses   165

Averaging down   172

Lessons learnt   175

Chapter 14. Adding to Existing Holdings   **177**

Changes in circumstances   178

Lessons learnt   180

Chapter 15. Selling Existing Holdings   **181**

Keeping calm   186

Tracking news announcements   190

Taking some profits   201

Lessons learnt   202

Chapter 16. Rights Issues and Placings   203

Right issues   203

Grandiose schemes   209

Rights issues at or near the market price   213

Placings and open offers   213

Special dividends and share buybacks   214

Lessons learnt   216

Chapter 17. Takeovers and Demergers   217

Takeovers   217

Demergers   224

Lessons learnt   228

Chapter 18. Costs and Taxes   229

Costs   229

Taxes   232

Chapter 19. An Example Portfolio   239

Shares bought   240

Portfolio valuation (at start)   242

Dividends received   243

Issues faced   243

Lessons learnt   247

Index   249

Preface

Who this book is for

Anyone who is thinking of investing, however much or however little, will benefit from the information, advice and guidance contained in these pages. Similarly those who already have a portfolio will find it helpful to stand back and assess whether they are making the most of their money and whether their portfolio is meeting their needs.

Many investors simply pick shares that take their fancy, or perhaps ones that have been recommenced in the financial press, without any thought for whether their selections create a suitable or balanced portfolio.

They then cling on to their purchases irrespective of whether their investment needs have changed or whether the companies they chose still meet their investment objectives.

This book explains in simple terms the criteria for picking shares, and for deciding which companies to retain and which to dump.

It is written in a clear, easy to follow style that will suit beginners and more experienced investors alike. It is packed with real case studies taken from actual stock market events and developments to illustrate the key points.

What this book covers

We are interested primarily in building and maintaining a portfolio of UK company shares.

These are not the only assets we may want to invest in and one of the recurring themes of this book is the merit of spreading investments to maximise our opportunities and minimise the risk of heavy losses.

We do look at other types of asset: Some, such as exchange traded funds and company bonds that are linked to the stock market, and others, such as commodities and property, that have their own economic cycles.

However, these assets are considered additions to a well-run share portfolio, with the investor taking a view on what they offer by way of diversifying risks. We consider the different risks and rewards that they offer compared with shares.

We also look briefly at the possibility of investing in overseas companies, either on the London Stock Exchange or on a foreign exchange such as New York or Tokyo.

The main thrust of this book, though, is investment in UK companies through the London stock market. This is an area that UK investors will be most familiar with and more comfortable with, where reliable information and knowledgeable analysis are most freely available.

We consider the different attitudes that investors should have, depending on whether they are investing for income or for growth, and help you decide which is right for you.

How this book is structured

The book is divided into three sections. Listed below are the three sections and the major topics covered within each section.

Part I: The choice of assets

- What types of asset are available to invest in
- The merits and pitfalls of various assets
- How to choose which assets suit you
- The importance of equities in any portfolio

Part II: Building a portfolio

- Deciding what you want from your portfolio

- Income versus growth

- Why you should diversify

- How to select shares

- How to choose between cyclical and defensive stocks

- How big a portfolio should you hold?

Part III: Managing your portfolio

- Monitoring your portfolio

- Active trading and investing for the long term

- Stop losses and share price averaging

- Rebalancing your portfolio

- Corporate actions: rights issues and takeovers

- Mitigating tax liabilities

Supporting website

The accompanying website for this book can be found at:
www.harriman-house.com/howtobuildashareportfolio

Introduction

When I wrote to a friend that I was writing books on stock market investing, he wrote back to say: "I hope you advise people to put their money under the mattress."

No, I do not!

Putting your money under the mattress is just plain stupid. Your cash deteriorates as inflation gnaws at its value – and you risk losing the lot if you are burgled. Even if you escaped the attentions of the criminal fraternity for 50 years or so, £1000 cash stuffed under the mattress in 1960 would be worth less than £60 at today's prices.

The only time that holding banknotes and coins would be worthwhile is in a prolonged period of deflation, when the amount of goods they could buy would increase. Since governments believe that modest inflation of 2-3% is good for the economy, we are not likely to see cash heaven in our lifetimes.

Stashing large amounts of money away in a savings account bearing near to zero interest is not much better. Again your cash loses value over time; and the bailout of banks around the world during the credit crisis demonstrates that even this form of investment is not entirely risk free.

There is a wide range of investments that offer income, capital gains, or both. Yes, they do carry some risks but, as we shall see, risk can be managed and minimised.

We shall also see that a sensibly constructed portfolio of shares in companies quoted on a reliable stock market such as the London Stock Exchange offers the best rewards combined with the least risk.

Prepare to get that cash out from under the mattress.

Part I
The Choice of Assets

Chapter 1.
The Range of Assets

What is a portfolio?

Let us start by defining what a portfolio is. We are talking about a range of investments held by one person or perhaps by a group of individuals such as a family or an investment club.

A portfolio investor thinks primarily about the total value of his portfolio (in a wider sense, we might call this his wealth). This may sound obvious, but it's a fact that many investors focus more on the success or failure of individual stocks rather than their total portfolio performance. It is, after all, very easy to dwell on the stock that rose 200% – or fell 90%. But in portfolio terms, these are secondary matters; it is the total portfolio value that is of prime importance. And this requires us to approach investing in a different way than just becoming obsessed with picking a winner every time.

So, the stocks we add to our portfolio are not just any old investments slung together from a range of privatisations or tips we've seen in Sunday newspapers. We are considering a sensible, disciplined approach in systematically assembling a range of assets that meet the criteria that we set for ourselves – criteria that balance the expected risks and rewards of our investments.

This is not a complicated procedure and you don't need a degree in mathematics to do it. Nor does it have to occupy every waking hour. Most of it is common sense and knowing what you want out of life. No two people would look for exactly the same portfolio and a portfolio assembled in your twenties would not be the same as one that meets your desires in retirement.

Building and maintaining a portfolio involves:

- selecting assets appropriate to your requirements

- deciding how much of each asset to buy

- striking and maintaining a balance

- setting targets for the performance of your portfolio

- measuring the portfolio's performance against a benchmark such as the FTSE index.

Questions to ask before you start

But there are important questions you must ask yourself before you consider any kind of investment.

First, write down in one column all your household's monthly income and in a second column your total monthly expenditure, including any mortgage payments, utility bills, average credit card bills and so on. This will give you a clear idea of your finances and how much you can comfortably invest.

Now, the questions:

- *Do you own your home?*
  This should probably be your first investment, if you have the initial deposit that gets you on the housing ladder. You have to live somewhere and houses tend to rise in value over time.

- *Do you have some cash that you can get at easily in an emergency?*
  If you tie up all your money in investments you may find yourself scrambling to sell assets at unfavourable prices, so do keep something by for a rainy day.

- *Are you looking primarily for capital growth or income?*

- *How long do you want to lock your capital away for?*

- *How averse are you to taking risks?*

These are questions that only you can answer.

Even if you invest through a financial adviser or pay for advice from your stockbroker, only you know how you feel in your heart of hearts. No investment is worth having sleepless nights over.

If you do have cash to invest, though, there is a wide range of investments available to you. This book argues that a sound portfolio of equities is the best option, although there is absolutely no reason why investors should not widen their portfolios to include other forms of investment. After all, variety is a way of spreading risk.

While this book is primarily about building a share portfolio, it is worth quickly taking a look at the alternatives. In doing so we may come to a greater appreciation of the merits of shares as an investment and, perhaps, decide that sticking with shares is the soundest policy.

Let's start by considering the various asset classes that are readily available.

Shares

We will look at shares in detail in the following chapter, so here I will just make a few quick points.

Quite simply, no other investment offers you the many advantages you will find in holding a portfolio of shares; no other investment provides the combination of income and capital gains that shares do. Shares in sound, profitable companies will gain value over time and dividends will increase, so your capital and your income both rise to beat inflation.

No other investment offers you the sheer variety that shares do. You can:

- buy for the short, medium or long term, or build a mixture of all three, and change your mind whenever you want

- stick to dull but safe companies or chance your arm with high fliers

- collect a range of varied companies so you stand to gain whatever the economic circumstances

- take advantage of concessions on income, capital gains and inheritance taxes

- enjoy perks for shareholders in a range of companies including travel, retail and even housebuilding

- easily check how your investments are faring in your daily newspaper or online

- invest at home or abroad, and pick foreign stocks through the London Stock Exchange

- choose investments in developed, growing and emerging economies

- trade on well regulated, orderly stock markets.

It is true that, as the old mantra puts it, shares can go down as well as up. Companies can and do go bust. What is more, dividends on ordinary shares can be reduced or scrapped in tough times.

The answer is to spread your investments across a range of shares in different sectors so that one bad apple does not ruin the harvest.

Cash

The judicious use of a cash pile has its merits:

- It will normally earn interest, however little, when deposited with a bank or building society and you can choose whether to have instant access to it or tie it up for a longer period in return for extra interest. At least you are getting some return.

- Getting some return on your cash will make you feel more comfortable with staying out of the stock market when you cannot see a worthwhile company to invest in. During a bear market you may wish to stay out of shares until the market settles. During a bull run you may wish to take profits and wait to buy back at lower levels.

- It provides you with a source of instant funds if you suddenly incur a hefty expense, avoiding the need to cash in shares or other assets when it may not be convenient to do so.

Many people of all ages think that money in a deposit account at the bank is safer than investing in shares. Yet the opposite is nearer to the truth.

Your savings deposit gradually loses value as it is eroded by inflation. You may be able to live off the interest now but that interest will be worth less and less as inflation reduces the real value of the pound.

When interest rates are high, so too is inflation, so your deposit is being washed away at alarming speed; when inflation is low your savings retain their value for longer but the interest is reduced, as many pensioners discovered after the Bank of England slashed its base rate to just 0.5%, with banks reducing the rates for savers to as little as 0.1%.

Gold

The precious metal is an unusual form of investment for many reasons, not least that it is dug from the ground at considerable expense, refined at further expense, moulded into ingots again at a cost and then buried back underground in bank vaults, where it is stored at more expense in security and insurance premiums.

In practical terms it is pretty useless as a store of wealth because of its sheer weight, as you cannot take it with you if your cache is under threat. Mind you, it is hard to steal for the same reason.

The more highly refined it is, the more value it has as a store of wealth. However, gold is also used in jewellery and dentistry, for instance, where its value increases if it is of lower purity because the metal is very soft and wears away easily.

A little gold can go a remarkably long way, as any user of gold leaf will tell you. Yet a small amount will weigh more than you can carry.

No wonder kings and commoners have been fascinated by this weird and wonderful element since time immemorial.

The gold standard

For many years gold was used to determine the value of currencies, initially because coins were minted from it and then because each currency was valued against one ounce of gold – the gold standard.

In the 1940s and 50s the price of gold was fixed at $34 an ounce, but the dollar came under pressure in the 1960s as speculators realised that the US government did not have enough reserves to maintain the formal link. Gold was re-valued up to $35, then $38, then $44 an ounce before the price was allowed to float in 1973.

The freeing of the dollar from the gold standard has distorted the price of gold over the period since. Initially, gold soared to $850 in 1980 as the buying frenzy fed on itself. Then it collapsed below $400 as demand was sated and the metal fell out of fashion as an investment must-have.

The 20 years marking the end of the millennium were particularly disappointing for gold addicts. Eventually the price bottomed at $295 in January 2000.

Since 2000, gold has come back into fashion with investors. The three-year bear market for shares that greeted the turn of the century, the sight of planes crashing into the Twin Towers in New York, the war to oust Saddam Hussein that sucked the US and UK into long years of attrition in Iraq and Afghanistan and the sub-prime scandal that precipitated banking collapses and the credit crunch all sent nervous investors into a search for a safe haven.

The precious metal topped $1000 an ounce in 2009 and reached a peak just above $1200 in December that year. While the momentum was maintained, the talk was not of taking substantial profits but of the price reaching $1500.

Figure 1.1: Price of gold (1968–2010)

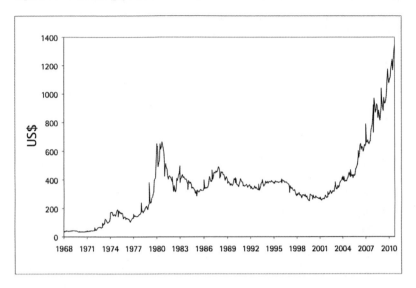

Gold has two aspects to its price

Firstly, there is the truly commercial value set by supply and demand. Gold miners produce the stuff and end users make necklaces, false teeth and the like. As with any commodity, if production outstrips demand, the price will fall; if production falls short of demand then the price will rise.

About 70% of the world's gold is used in jewellery so this is an important factor in keeping up the price of gold. It costs more than $400 an ounce to mine gold. If the price drops below this level, mining it will not be economically worthwhile and supply will dwindle until the price rises again.

Secondly, there is the (possibly conflicting) pull of sentiment. Gold is traditionally seen as a safe haven in times of conflict or uncertainty in the currency market. Tension in the Middle East or a run on the dollar sends the price of gold soaring, while peaceful periods ease the pressure on the gold price.

Another factor, though, has come into play in recent years. Investing in gold has become fashionable again. The price has risen slowly but surely over several years, each dollar on the price serving to persuade new and existing investors that it is a solid investment where you cannot lose if you hold on for the long term.

Such an impression is, however, flawed. There are clear disadvantages in investing in gold.

- There is just one type of gold, so you cannot spread the risk as you can with shares. It is true that you could buy gold coins rather than ingots but the value will move in the same direction whatever form of gold you buy.

- The price of gold could drop back as quickly as it has risen if it falls out of favour. The price has in fact been quite volatile over time.

- It pays no dividend, as companies do to shareholders. Your only possible gain is a capital gain from a rising price.

- You are unlikely to want to keep a store of gold locked in your house. If you did take physical delivery of the stuff you would have to insure it, which eats away at your capital.

There is a sensible alternative to buying gold direct and that is to invest in a fund that specialises in gold by buying the metal itself or holding shares in companies involved in precious metals.

Gilts

Gilt-edged securities are bonds issued by the government. They hold two major attractions: they are relatively safe and there is a wide variety to choose from.

Since they are issued by the government, gilts are seen as the safest form of investment in the UK because, after all, if the government goes bust then we are all up the creek anyway.

As with shares, however, the value of gilts can fall as well as rise. In times of rising interest rates, the price of gilts falls to give, in effect, a higher rate on each £100 invested, while if interest rates fall the price of gilts rises.

A disadvantage of gilts compared with shares is that, with the exception of a handful of government bonds that are linked to the rate of inflation, the interest rate is fixed so there is no prospect of seeing your income increase year by year. Also capital gains are limited because gilts have a fixed redemption price – or no redemption price at all in the case of undated gilts.

It is possible to buy bonds issued by foreign governments but this can be dangerous. Argentina defaulted on $100 billion worth of debt in December 2001. It was not the first time that a Latin American country had defaulted, nor even the first time that Argentina had, but it was the most spectacular. More recently the credit crunch crisis cast doubts over the sovereign debt of Greece and other Mediterranean countries.

Investors should bear in mind that gilt purchases work extremely well if you buy at the top of the interest rate cycle because you have locked in a good rate of interest and stand to make a capital gain on top. You are doomed to disappointment if you buy gilts just before interest rates start to rise because the value of your holding will fall.

Gilts are traded on a liquid market so there is no difficulty in buying and selling them. If you choose to hold gilts alongside a shares portfolio you are providing yourself with a known level of income to offset the less certain payment of company dividends, which can be reduced in hard times.

Summary: gilts are attractive when interest rates are high, which is when shares tend to be out of favour.

Company bonds

These have the same characteristics as gilts except that they are issued by companies rather than the government. They are thus seen as carrying a higher risk of default than gilts and they will carry a higher interest rate to compensate.

The larger and more secure the company, the smaller the interest rate gap will be over gilts.

Bonds do represent an alternative way of investing in sound companies but you do not own a stake in the company as you do with shares. Also the interest rate is static while you hope that dividends on shares will rise over time.

Property

Buy-to-let became highly popular before the credit crunch. It was fuelled in particular by loans from Bradford & Bingley – one of the many building societies that turned into a bank and needed to find a niche within the financial sector. Bradford & Bingley had issued a quarter of the one million buy-to-let mortgages in operation when the UK housing market collapsed in the first half of 2008.

While there is much merit in buying your own home, since you have to live somewhere and you might as well pay the rent money into a mortgage instead, buying houses and flats to rent out is not such a clear cut winner as was supposed.

The main drawback of investing in property is that you need a fair chunk of cash, even assuming that you can get a mortgage to cover most of the cost. You will also be taxed on the income from your investment and on any capital gains you make when you sell.

And there is another problem: it may be difficult to sell if you want to cash in your investment. There may not be a ready supply of buyers falling over themselves to buy you out.

Finding the right tenant also presents difficulties. You need to buy in an area where people want to rent, which may not be where you would want to own property. Any damage to property or furnishings is likely to come out of your pocket and the tenants may prove unable or unwilling to pay the rent, in which case it is expensive and time consuming to evict them.

On the other hand, property does tend to offer one of the virtues of shares: if all goes well you enjoy income while the value of your investment rises to offset inflation. If you are unlucky and the value of your investment falls then at least you have had some income as compensation along the way and you will not lose everything, unless the house falls down.

Works of art

This is another area that has moved in and out of fashion. It is true that valuable paintings, sculpture and the like can appreciate heavily in value; but you really do have to be an expert to do well.

Disadvantages include the cost of insurance, the vagaries of the market place and the substantial commissions that auction houses charge. If you buy and sell at auction you will find that prices for similar objects can vary enormously according to whether there are competing bids.

Collectibles

The popularity of TV programmes featuring people who have found valuable items in the loft or at a car boot sale and sold them for a small fortune has alerted investors to the possibility of establishing collections of Dinky toys, cigarette cards and Giles annuals to be sold on to avid enthusiasts.

The emergence of auction websites such as eBay has made trading easier and more popular. Online auctions are cheaper than salerooms and you are more likely to drum up a competitive auction.

Postage stamps and coins are perennially popular, though most people grow out of this childhood phase. It can admittedly be a lucrative pastime. According to Stanley Gibbons, the most famous name in stamp collecting, stamps increased in value at a compound annual rate of 13.2% over the ten years from 1998 to 2008, rising in value even after the start of the credit crunch.

There was, however, no reason to believe that such strong growth would continue: this was one case of believing that the past is no guide to the future. Indeed, the faster an asset of this type has risen in the recent past, the more reason there is to think that a correction is imminent.

Collectible items have no value in themselves. They do not make profits as companies do and thus depend entirely on new collectors joining in. Many collectors become sentimentally attached to their wares, so that far from cashing in profits they simply hang on irrespective of how the market is doing.

Tastes change and this year's fad may not be in demand next year. Also you are likely to be spending considerable time scouring boot sales and charity shops with limited success.

Funds

It is not necessary to assume the whole burden of selecting shares onto your own shoulders if you are not confident. Most banks offer ISA investments that put your money into funds investing in the stock market. Most popular are the ones that buy shares in the FTSE 100 index comprising the 100 largest companies listed on the London Stock Exchange as these are seen in the main as safe, solid enterprises.

Such multi-million pound funds can spread your money across a much wider range of shares than you could achieve yourself with your modest assets and thus are correspondingly safer.

Some funds are permanently available while others have a short period in which you can subscribe and are then closed. Ask your bank what is available or ask to see an investment adviser. Remember that you do not have to go to the bank where you have your current account although you may be more comfortable doing so.

Most likely the financial adviser will offer only the bank's own products so the range will be limited. Don't be afraid to ask if this is the case.

Make sure that the adviser fully understands what you want from your investments and what your attitude is to risk. The adviser needs to know your personal financial circumstances in order to offer you the best advice.

There is no need to sign up on the spot. Take literature home with you and sleep on it. Read what you are given thoroughly and carefully and do not hesitate to ask about anything that troubles you.

IFAs

Alternatively you can invest through an independent financial adviser (IFA). As the name implies, the adviser works for him or herself and is not tied to just one range of financial products. The difficulty is finding one you feel comfortable with. Look for names under Financial Advisers in your local telephone directory. They will all be regulated by the Financial Services Authority. Ask your friends if they use an IFA whom they can recommend.

IFAs earn a living by taking a commission from the funds that they put your money into. The advantage is that you get their services free but it does mean that they can be tempted to suggest those funds that pay them the highest commission. You can get round this by agreeing to pay the adviser a set fee out of your own money with any commission being added to your investment. Make sure the basis of payment for your IFA is clearly agreed right at the start.

However, there is no reason why you should not invest in shares yourself if you follow a few simple rules. After all, you know your needs and aspirations better than anyone else ever could.

Exchange Traded Funds

New on the scene are Exchange Traded Funds (ETFs) which invest in a range of assets such as the FTSE 100, in a commodity such as platinum or soya beans, or in corporate bonds. The value of the funds rises or falls in line with the underlying asset.

The funds are run by specialist companies in the same way as unit trusts or open-ended investment funds are, so there will be a management fee.

The main advantages of ETFs are:

- Very low costs

- You can spread risks across a wide range of shares and commodities

- They can be traded just like shares

- They do not trade at a discount to the value of the assets as investment trusts tend to do.

The fee will be lower than those charged by a conventional fund, typically around 0.35% which includes all expenses incurred in running the ETF. This is because ETFs are managed passively – the manager simply buys whatever investments are appropriate to the fund. With investment and unit trusts the manager is more active, attempting to buy the right shares at the right time to boost profits.

ETFs are traded on the stock exchange just like ordinary shares. You can buy and sell at any time during stock market hours and prices are determined by supply and demand in exactly the same way as share prices. Pricing is thus more transparent than with unit trusts, where the price of units is set once a day by the manager.

ETFs trade at the full aggregate value of their components, unlike investment trusts which usually trade at a discount of several percentage points to their underlying value.

These funds allow investors to spread their cash over a wider field than would be possible buying single shares one or two at a time. If you buy a FTSE 100 tracker – the most popular ETF in the UK, accounting for more than 15% of ETF turnover – you have exposure to all the 100 top shares in the UK at one go.

If events in the news are likely to affect a sector or a market, you can move swiftly in or out of a corresponding ETF accordingly.

They allow you to move into investments that you might otherwise have steered clear of, perhaps because you do not know enough about a particular type of investment or you do not know how to invest in it. Thus you are able to broaden your horizons with little risk.

So, for example, if you wanted to invest in metals but did not know how to go about it you can simply buy an ETF investing in the metals you think will rise in price.

Some ETFs allow you to 'short' the market, in other words to bet that values will fall. This is difficult for ordinary shareholders investing on the stock market.

Global spread of ETFs

ETFs have been particularly popular in the United States but have been slow to take off in the UK. You may find that there is not as wide a range of products or the depth of liquidity here as in the US. Nonetheless, the value of ETFs worldwide topped $1 trillion in 2009.

Investors may need to check exactly what is in a fund before they subscribe. For example, an ETF covering emerging markets may not invest in all emerging markets and will almost certainly invest more heavily in some than others. So you could, for example, be buying into China when you think that India offers better prospects.

Most ETFs traded on the London Stock Exchange are actually incorporated in Ireland and UK investors would not be eligible for the UK Financial Services Compensation Scheme, although it has to be said that the risk of default is very low.

ETFs that invest in volatile markets carry a serious risk of losing you money and those with investments priced in foreign currencies carry an exchange rate risk. If the pound falls, that's fine, but a rising pound would lower the value of your investment when translated back into sterling.

Summary comparison of assets

Table 1.1: The merits of rival investments

Type of investment	Advantages	Disadvantages
Bank or building society account	Deposit remains intact and interest provides income.	Value of investment is eroded by inflation and interest rates may fall.
Gilts	Backed by the government so minimal risk of default. Provide regular income.	Capital is eroded by inflation and value of investment can fall.
Company bonds and preference shares	Provide income and take precedence over ordinary shareholders if the company gets into financial trouble.	Do not share the benefits if the company does well. Capital is eroded by inflation.
Ordinary shares	Solid companies will increase dividends, pushing the share price higher, so capital and income rise to offset inflation.	Investment is wiped out if the company goes bust. Dividends can be reduced.
Investment and unit trusts	Gives you wide spread of investments and you benefit from experienced manager's expertise.	Management fees are deducted from your investment.
Exchange Traded Funds	Allow you to spread investments. Low management charges.	Passive investment so you lose flexibility.
Gold	Safe haven in a crisis; hedge against inflation.	Does not provide income; prices fluctuate.
Works of art/collectibles	Can often be picked up cheaply and sold for a large profit.	Do not provide income; selling can be expensive; fashions change.

Costs

Every investment comes at a price and you must earn enough from the investment to cover those costs before you start to make a profit.

Art

The most expensive form of investment is operating through auction houses. These charge vendors anything from 8% to 20% of the sale price. To add insult to injury, VAT is charged on the commission at the current rate, which is 20% from 4th January 2011, and there may be a small fee for putting an item into the auction irrespective of whether it is sold.

The buyer will also usually be charged 10% on the sale price VAT on the commission. If you buy an item for £1000 you need to sell it for at least £1230, and possibly as much as £1450, just to break even.

Using online auction sites is cheaper and you attract a potentially wider audience. For example, eBay has a sliding scale commission for buyers with a maximum of 5.25% plus a listing fee of no more than £2. You could buy and resell that £1000 item and make a profit at £1060.

Equities

In contrast, an online stock broker will execute an order to buy or sell shares for on average £12.50 per trade and in some cases for as little as £10 a time. Thus a £1000 share purchase will cost £10 plus 0.5% stamp duty of £5, Selling some time later at a cost of £10 makes a total cost of £25, so you need to sell your £1000 investment for £1025 to break even.

However, the bonus with a share portfolio is that if your £1000 worth of shares pays a dividend of £25 while you hold them, then you have covered your costs anyway.

These figures are particularly important the more actively you trade, since you will be running up costs several times over. For example, if you buy and sell a £1000 investment once a month for a year, the total cost will be around £300 (12 x £25) – which is a big chunk of the £1000 investment.

Gilts and bonds

Buying and selling gilts or company bonds can also be carried out through your broker at a similar flat rate fee.

If you choose to receive advice from your broker you will find yourself paying 1% to 3% of the value of your share trades as a fee and you will probably be required to carry out a minimum number of transactions.

Property

Costs of other types of investment vary enormously. Buying property will involve solicitor's fees of several hundred pounds, plus your mortgage lender's fees if you need to borrow money, plus stamp duty from 1% to 5% depending on the value of the property. Any rent received will have to cover mortgage repayments and repair and maintenance bills. When you sell there will be estate agents' bills.

The important point is that you should check what the costs will be with the broker/auctioneer/estate agent before you rush in, and you should be satisfied that you can cover them.

Mix and match

We have noted that different asset classes have different attributes and drawbacks. There is no reason why you should not combine two or more of them if that suits your investment needs. For instance, you could invest in a tracker fund for safety and stability while running your own share portfolio. At least you would then know whether you were as good as the professionals!

You may fancy your chances as a property landlord but not want to put all your eggs into this basket. You could buy one property to see how it works out and put the rest of your surplus cash into dividend-paying shares. Cash from the dividends could help to tide you over if you have a period without a tenant.

Why build a properly constructed portfolio?

So, you have decided to invest, but perhaps you are wondering why you should bother putting together a structured portfolio. Why not just buy whatever takes your fancy?

No-one is stopping you. If your instincts are good and you can spot a winner when you see one, by all means go ahead and follow your nose. Best of luck.

You will certainly need luck, however good you are as a tipster. You will end up with investments that may or may not meet your needs. You will almost certainly overload your portfolio with too many companies from one sector as each initial success prompts you to choose more of the same. You are also likely to overstretch your finances as you pile in merrily whenever you spot the next racing certainty.

This is the mind of a gambler, not an investor.

Alternatively, you may want to go to the other extreme. Fearing your propensity to make poor choices, you could opt to put your savings into a fund such as a unit or investment trust.

This again is a perfectly legitimate investment strategy, though an ultra-cautious one. You do at least have some choice between funds that invest for income and those that invest for capital gains. However, you are entirely in the hands of the fund manager and have no say in the investment decisions.

Tracker funds are an especially useful way for beginners to get into the habit of stock market investing and if you are nervous why not run a tracker fund alongside your own investment portfolio? This is, a strategy that many experienced investors follow.

Lessons learnt

You need to do a bit of serious thinking before you start to invest:

- How much can I really afford to invest?

- What do I want at this stage in my life?

- What investment or investments best meet those needs?

You should consider equities as your preferred choice, either on their own or in tandem with other asset classes, because:

- They are comparatively cheap to buy and to hold

- They offer the prospect of income and capital gains

- They are in the main traded on properly regulated exchanges.

Now it is time to start building your portfolio.

Chapter 2.
The Attractions of Equities

Performance

While one should be cautious of statistics, since they can be often be twisted to suit any argument, there is a strong statistical case for investing in shares over time. According to the Credit Suisse Global Investment Returns Yearbook 2010, if you invested £100 in 1900 and reinvested the dividends you would have amassed £28,690 by 2010 even after allowing for inflation. Had you invested in bonds instead, you would have ended up with just £430 now. And gilts are no better than company bonds.

Note that the actual figures would have been considerably greater given the rampant inflation of the 1960s and 1970s. This is the gain you would have made in addition to the rate of inflation.

Figure 2.1: Chart showing long term equity gains

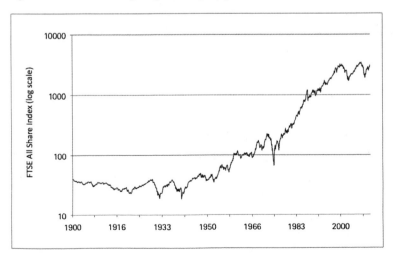

The return on equities has been 5.3% a year on top of inflation, while the real return[1] on bonds has been 1.3%.

OK, so we weren't around in 1900, when most people did not have cash to invest anyway. What about more recent years? The picture is arguably not so good.

Barclays study

The Barclays Equity Gilt Study 2009 found:

> "Equity investors have been on a wild and ultimately disappointing ride over the past decade. Equities have been the worst-performing asset class since 1997, sharply underperforming all other asset classes."

Oh dear.

Barclays calculated that the return on UK equities between 1998 and 2008 was a measly 1.05%. After allowing for the effects of inflation, shareholdings fell in value by 1.5% in real terms over the 10 years. Only 1964-74 was a worse decade – thanks to the 73% collapse in share prices at the end of that period caused by the quadrupling of crude oil prices. It was not just a case of the UK lagging behind the world. US equities fell in value by 0.3% a year over the period 1998-2008. Again, inflation made matters worse. Only the 1930s produced a worse performance in the US.

So are the golden days of equities consigned to history?

Not a bit of it.

As the Barclays report says:

> "The weak returns from equities over the past decade are not due to some intrinsic problem with the asset class. Rather, they are attributable to the extreme overvaluation of equities at the start of the decade."

---

[1] Real return is the return after accounting for inflation.

Equity markets in the UK, the US, Japan, Europe and elsewhere had been on an upward trend since 1982, reaching record levels in the process. The boom of telecom and technology stocks at the end of the millennium was the very thick layer of icing on the cake and it propelled market indices to unrealistic levels.

When technology companies with no record of producing profits began to cave in on themselves, the Goldilocks years of steady growth, not too hot and not too cold, were put to flight by three bearish years. However, there was nothing wrong with equities in general. The stock market was just painfully returning to normality.

From March 2003 onwards much of the lost ground was made up before the global credit crunch of 2008 onwards took its toll.

Overpriced equities

The Barclays study is at pains to point out that corporate profits continued to grow but,

> "investors were paying a very high premium to access these profits at the start of the decade."

The study remarks:

> "From 1997 through to 2002, equities were valued at unusually expensive levels relative to earnings and corporate net worth. The collapse in equities after 2001 partially corrected this overvaluation, as equity prices declined by more than earnings during the 2001-3 global slowdown."

The subsequent economic boom of 2003-8 generated a strong trend in profitability and in turn generated a strong rally in stock markets. When the surge in growth ended abruptly in 2008, equity prices fell in line with profits.

So the lesson is not to shun shares, which over the longer term will offer better returns than other forms of investment. The message is that shares can and do sometimes trade at way above their real value and that you should look to buy in at the bottom of the market –

not, as small investors so often do, charge in at the peak after watching City professionals rake in all the profits.

The importance of measuring total return

It is very tempting to measure the performance of our portfolio by looking at changes in share prices. This is less than half the picture. We should look at total returns, a value that adds dividends received to share price changes.

As an example, the Rathbone Income Fund saw the value of its share portfolio rise by 40% in the first ten years of the millennium, but income from reinvesting dividends added another 79%, making a total return over ten years of 119%.

Over the same period the FTSE All-Share index fell by 8% but that was more than wiped out by a 40% return in dividends, giving a total return of 32%.

Diversification

Apart from income and capital gains, shares offer us diversification, which means we can spread our risk. Assuming we invest in a range of companies in a range of sectors we would have to be extremely unlucky, as well as remarkably poor investors, if we found all the companies we picked were wiped out.

The wider the range of companies we choose, the more we reduce the overall risk of our portfolio that results from exposure to problems at specific companies. And the greater the possibility that we pick a few star winners along the way.

The Buffett argument against diversification

It is only fair to say that Warren Buffett, the chairman of investment fund Berkshire Hathaway and the man dubbed as the Sage of Omaha, has argued against diversification. In so doing he disregarded the view of many pundits, perhaps the majority of investment experts, that diversification reduces risk.

He argued in 1993:

> "We believe that a policy of portfolio concentration may well decrease risk if it raises, as it should, both the intensity with which an investor thinks about a business and the comfort-level he must feel with its economic characteristics before buying into it."

In other words, the fewer shares you buy the more carefully you study the companies you are buying into and the more comfortable you have to feel with each investment. You are thus forced to take fewer risks.

Buffett has further argued that diversification is 'a protection against ignorance'.

If you have little idea about investing, you need to spread your portfolio wider because you lack the ability to spot good prospects, his theory goes. The wider portfolio thus gives you a better chance of picking up top-performing companies to balance out the poor ones.

In contrast, diversification makes very little sense for those who know what they are doing because they will choose excellent investments and thus have little need to spread the risk.

As he put it rather colourfully:

> "If you understand the business, you don't need to own very many of them. If you have a harem of 40 women, you never get to know any of them very well."

The counterargument

One is reluctant to contradict such a successful investor as Warren Buffett and, indeed, he is right in principle. We would rather invest in four great companies than in four great companies, four moderately successful ones and four poor performers.

The trouble is that Buffett has:

- plenty of time to study the companies he considers investing in

- the financial clout to gain access to chief executives and chairmen of companies he might invest in

- build large shareholdings that give him influence over strategic decisions at companies he does invest in

- the financial resources to tide him over if he makes a poor investment.

By contrast, we ordinary mortals have other things to do with our lives. And yes, let's admit it, we do not have the financial knowledge, acumen and experience that Buffett has.

If you have the time and skill to always back really tip-top companies then go ahead and restrict your investments Buffet-style. Otherwise there is considerable merit in spreading the load to avoid the risk of being stuck with two or three underperforming companies.

In any case, Buffett does not always practise what he preaches. In mid-2008 his Berkshire Hathaway investment company reported that it held shares in 39 US publicly traded companies.

Admittedly ten of them accounted for 80% of the value of the portfolio; but ten companies is often recommended by pundits as an ideal size of portfolio for a modest investor. Ten companies are numerous enough to spread risk and few enough for you to spare the time to keep an eye on them.

Foreign stocks

On the whole it is best to stick with what you know and understand. For most investors that means investing in the UK. With more than 2000 companies to choose from on the two London Stock Exchange boards – the main board and the less heavily regulated Alternative Investment Market – there is ample choice.

And most of the largest UK-based companies are truly international. Nearly 70% of the profits of FTSE 100 index members is earned abroad: in other words, for every £1 they earn in the UK they make £2 overseas, in developed and emerging nations across the continents and across a broad spectrum of sectors. They include:

- banks such as Barclays with operations in the US and HSBC in Asia

- oil companies including BP drilling and refining oil around the world

- insurance companies like Prudential with fast growing operations in the Far East

- telecoms giant Vodafone with a global spread.

In any case, investing purely in London does open up the opportunity to invest in foreign companies as many have chosen to be listed over here. There is nothing suspicious about this. The London stock market offers much greater liquidity than its counterparts in many other parts of the world and it is therefore often easier to raise money in a listing here rather than back home.

Foreign stocks that are or have been members of the FTSE 100 index include:

- **Kazakhmys**, a metals and power generation group based in Kazakhstan

- **Carnival**, the American cruise line company that bought P&O Princess

- **Eurasian Natural Resources**, another Kazakhstan mining group

- **BHP Billiton**, the global mining group based in Australia

- **Antofagasta**, a copper miner in Chile

- **Fresnillo**, yet another mining company, this time specialising in precious metals in Mexico.

One might be inclined to add Royal Dutch Shell, steel maker Corus and household goods group Unilever, all Anglo-Dutch enterprises, or Asian-oriented bank Standard Chartered, to that list.

The AIM market has become particularly attractive for foreign companies based in countries without a well established junior market.

Advantages of looking abroad

One advantage of investing in foreign companies with listings in London is that you widen your portfolio to include companies with less exposure to the UK economy, thus giving your portfolio more breadth. If Asian economies do well when the UK is struggling you have winners to offset your poorly performing UK shares.

We saw during the credit crunch that HSBC and Standard Chartered, two banks with heavy Asian commitments, fared better than RBS and Lloyds with greater UK exposure.

If you want to include a mining company in your portfolio you should certainly consider foreign-based ones because of the shortage of suitable UK companies in this sector. As we saw in the list above, several of the largest foreign mining companies are listed on the LSE so there is no shortage of choice.

Another advantage in picking foreign companies with UK listings is that their shares are normally quoted in sterling, so you do not have to take foreign exchange fluctuations into account in keeping track of the performance of your shares.

However, we should not assume that it is necessarily the top flight foreign companies that come here. You should do your research before investing just as we would with a UK company. Indeed, you should be more cautious as you are less likely to understand foreign-based companies, foreign laws and foreign ways of doing business.

If in doubt, stay clear.

Case study: Antofagasta

Based in Chile, Antofagasta is a copper miner that sprang to the attention of investors as the price of metals rose during the pre-credit crunch boom. As long as the copper price holds up everything is fine. But this is very much a cyclical stock with the disadvantage of having basically one source of income from mining in one country.

Copper was above $8000 a tonne before the collapse of Lehman Brothers in 2008 spooked the markets and threatened a global recession. From a peak of $8730 that year, copper plunged to $2845 in December 2008. However, the price crossed back above $8000 in April 2010 thanks mainly to economic optimism in the US on the back of positive jobs data and after Chinese manufacturing figures came in stronger than expected.

There were admittedly lingering concerns about whether the copper price would stay within sight of its 2008 peak but the fundamentals of the copper market remained tight with the expectation that demand would exceed supply in 2011 as the global economic recovery gathered pace.

The recession prompted most producers to slash investment in new mines so any rise in demand was likely to create a shortage in supply. With its strong balance sheet, Antofagasta was able to continue to invest throughout the downturn and it expected to be able to increase production by almost 60% over the two years to mid-2012, taking full advantage of the higher copper price.

Figure 2.2: Antofagasta

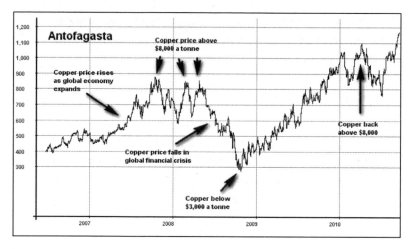

The company continued to have substantial cash reserves on its balance sheet, so a special dividend of 14 cents a share was paid in June 2010 on top of the 9.4 cents total of ordinary dividends for 2009-10.

Even after the dividend payments Antofagasta had net cash of about $1.4 billion and analysts expected this to rise to $2.6 billion by the end of 2010, raising hopes of another special dividend the following year.

An earthquake in Chile early in 2010 mercifully had little impact on the group's operations although it did offer a warning signal of what could go wrong. In this instance there was a 24-hour power cut at Antofagasta's Los Pelambres mine when an electricity substation was damaged but production was back to normal within three days.

Expansion at Antofagasta's Esperanza project, also in Chile, was expected to lead to the production of gold with a target of 270,000 ounces a year from 2011. This would bring a welcome second product into the equation, though not a new country.

Investing through overseas stock exchanges

The UK stock market offers many fine companies to invest in but by restricting yourself exclusively to London-quoted shares you could be missing out on a whole other world of potentially profitable overseas investing opportunities.

The decline of the British motor industry means we have no quoted automotive companies and a dearth of vehicle parts makers, with only GKN and TT Electronics springing readily to mind. If you want to invest in this sector you need to look at New York or Tokyo for a decent range of options.

Similarly the US and Japan have a wider range of information technology stocks than exists in the UK.

The US has the largest economy in the world, and has by far the largest and most active stock market with over 8000 companies to choose from. It is also home to some of the largest companies in the world; truly global companies with the added advantage that you will have heard of many of them and have some idea what they do.

They include technology giants Microsoft and Apple, retail chain Wal-Mart Stores which owns Asda supermarkets in the UK, General Electric Company and fast food purveyor McDonald's. You can even benefit from Warren Buffett's investment acumen by buying a stake in his Berkshire Hathaway investment company.

Note: As with every reference to individual shares in this book, do not take this as a recommendation to buy these particular shares. They are named just to give a flavour of the potential of the New York Stock Exchange.

Other stock markets

Other well regulated markets you may wish to consider are Paris, Milan, Amsterdam, Brussels and Frankfurt spread across Western Europe. Within the Pacific area, Tokyo and Hong Kong are the best known markets. Australia also has a stock market based in Sydney although the best known mining companies there are listed in London as well.

Asian markets are eight or nine hours ahead of us and are winding down as we start up. European stock markets open at 8am our time and trade until 4:30pm as we do in London. New York opens at 2:30pm our time so we can trade for most of the day and evening if we so wish.

One disadvantage of investing on foreign exchanges is that your broker may not be willing to offer you dealing facilities for them and will charge higher dealing costs if trading is possible.

However, there is no stamp duty paid on US and European stocks so you recoup the extra charge when buying.

Lessons learnt

- Shares offer a wide range of investment opportunities
- You can invest for capital gains, income or both
- You can easily tailor your portfolio to meet your investment needs
- You do not have to take risks to make money
- You can invest in UK stocks or in companies based abroad.

Part II
Building a Portfolio

Chapter 3.
Basic Decisions

Your first decision must be: what do you want from your share portfolio?

The basic choice is between investing for income to live off now and storing up wealth to be drawn on some time in the future.

The older you are, the more likely you are to want income, which you receive by way of dividends. If you have retired, are out of work or have a long term illness, a regular source of income is welcome on top of your pension or unemployment benefit.

Younger people, especially if in steady employment, have longer term considerations. You live on your wage and store up a nest egg.

Investing for income

Look for solid companies that make a profit and pay a dividend, especially if the company has a *progressive* dividend policy – that is it raises the dividend each year. You want companies that have the dividend well covered by earnings year after year.

Look for shares with a yield that is higher than inflation. The higher the yield, the more income you get. But beware: a company with a very high yield may be shunned by investors because of fears that trading has deteriorated and the dividend could be scrapped.

On the whole you will want to buy shares and hold them long term, taking full advantage of the ISA allowances. You should not be too worried if share prices fall because you are not looking to sell as long as your investments provide you with an income.

Your only reason to switch shares is if you are fully invested and you see a better prospect than one you currently hold. As you will not be looking for new companies to invest in you are less likely to benefit from paying for advice from your broker.

Investing for growth

You can still look for shares paying dividends because these are likely to appreciate in value and give capital gains as well. The dividends can be reinvested, either in the same company or in new investments.

However, here you are looking to be a more active and shorter term trader and you may wish to pay for investment advice.

Your best bet is to buy shares cheaply and sell after they have appreciated. You will be more inclined to get out if share prices fall and to take a loss on a particular investment rather than hang on with fingers crossed.

You will be more interested in the price/earnings ratio than the yield as you will be quite happy for the company to keep investing in the business, rather than handing the cash back to shareholders, for as long as it is successful.

You will not be too bothered about using an ISA but you might as well put any longer term investments into one as you are likely to exceed your capital gains allowance.

Our table sums up the basic differences between the two types of investor. We shall look at both attitudes to investment in the following chapters.

Table 3.1: Summary table of income and growth investing

Income	Growth
Long term investor	Shorter term investor
Less active investor	Active investor
Yield is priority	Price/earnings ratio is priority
Spend the dividends	Reinvest dividends
Less likely to need advice	More interested in analysts' research

How many?

Having decided on our basic strategy, we need to decide how many different companies to invest in and how many shares to buy in each.

Your initial aim should be to build a portfolio of between six and a dozen companies. How quickly you do this will depend on your circumstances, namely whether you have a lump sum to invest immediately or whether you intend to commit a certain amount each month from regular income.

The sensible approach is to decide how much cash you are realistically going to be investing over the next 12 months and take it from there.

Remember that if you are investing through the internet and paying a flat rate per transaction you should try to stake your entire commitment to each company in one go. If you buy through a traditional stock broker charging a percentage of the overall cost of the transaction, you can split sales in each individual company over a longer period of time without incurring more costs, assuming that you meet the broker's minimum transaction charge each time.

Lump sum

This is the easiest choice. Divide the money evenly between the shares that you select.

However, if you feel that one or two companies offer the brightest prospects then you can obviously allocate more money to these than to the others.

Conversely, you may fear that one company may underperform the rest. In this case do *not* allocate less money to this one investment: ditch it altogether. Find something better or re-divide the cash among the companies you do have faith in.

Lump sum followed by regular investments

Allocating resources is a bit trickier with this approach. Pick two or three companies for your initial investment, allocating this first batch of funds to the best prospects. Then, as more funds become available, spread your portfolio across more companies one at a time until you have a sufficiently wide range.

Once you have a balanced portfolio you can then consider whether to use further funds to widen the portfolio or to build up existing holdings. At this stage you should compare any proposed new investment with the current contents of your portfolio to see if it offers better prospects. If not, add to what you have got.

Regular investments

Invest in one company at a time, taking the best prospects first. You will not have a balanced portfolio initially but one investment a month will give you 12 companies within a year.

In selecting the order of purchases, bear in mind that you should favour any company that you think will do particularly well in the short term. There is no point in waiting until you have missed the boat. Also try to invest in different sectors in the early stages of investing so that you keep your portfolio as balanced as possible.

Each time you invest, reassess whether any companies you had previously ignored have since emerged with enhanced prospects. Be prepared to change your mind about your next investment if the argument is compelling.

Pounds, not numbers

When you make a purchase, you will have to decide how many shares to buy or how much to spend on each individual company.

Selling generally does not present the same problem, as you will be limited by the size of your holding – you will obviously not be able to sell more shares than you have bought. The likelihood is that you will have decided to sell your entire holding in a particular company, though you will have the option of selling part of your stake and retaining a smaller holding. We will look later in the chapter at why you might do this.

Because share prices vary enormously, you should think in terms of buying a similar value of shares in each company rather than a similar number. For example, supposing you bought 1000 shares in retailer Laura Ashley and 1000 shares in merchant bank Schroders on 28th June 2010.

At 12.75p a share, you would invest only £127.50 in Laura Ashley. At 1271p, your Schroders purchase would set you back £12,710. This is by no means an extreme example.

Putting around £1270 into each company would have given you 100 Schroders shares and 10,000 Laura Ashley shares.

It would be perfectly sensible to take an investment decision to put a larger amount into Schroders rather than Laura Ashley, but think in terms of pounds, not numbers of shares.

Sectors

The London Stock Exchange classifies companies into sectors according to the type of business they are in. Examples of these sectors are Aerospace and Defence; Banks; Beverages; Chemicals;

Electricity; Financial Services; Food Producers; General Retailers; Leather Goods; Oil and Gas Producers; Support Services; and Travel and Leisure.

A full list can be found by logging onto the exchange's website (**www.londonstockexchange.com**) and clicking on list of company sectors.

This is not an exact science and occasionally companies are reclassified, sometimes at their own request, when the nature of their business changes. To make matters more complicated, newspapers have their own classifications that may not match exactly with those of the exchange.

Thus model trains and racing cars maker Hornby counts as Leisure Goods on the LSE but as Household Goods in the *Daily Telegraph*!

In some cases similar companies may be in different sectors. Barratt Developments and Kier both build houses but Barratt is purely a housebuilder and comes under Household Goods and Home Construction while Kier has wider interests in construction and support services so it is slotted into Construction and Materials.

Where a company straddles two sectors it will generally be classified in the one where it makes most of its sales. In cases where a company has several diverse activities it will be classed as a Conglomerate.

Use sector classifications as a flexible rather than a rigid guide. When you consider adding a company to your portfolio, check what it actually does and consider whether it overlaps with any other company you have already invested in.

Weightings

We have already discussed the merits of diversifying by having a spread of companies and sectors within our portfolio and we should also give careful consideration to how much we invest in each type of business.

We do not have to hold the same number of shares in each company and we could invest in two or more companies in a sector that we felt had particularly good prospects. These are conscious decisions we should make, as overweighting investments into one sector is fine if that sector is doing well, but we will suffer disproportionately if circumstances change.

The weightings in your portfolio will inevitably change over time as some companies perform better than others. Say you have 10 shares in your portfolio and you put roughly equal amounts of cash into each. Then each investment will constitute 10% of your portfolio.

As the better performing shares rise in value they will come to represent a greater percentage of your portfolio. If you have invested in more than one company from a particular sector that has done well you may find that this sector occupies a larger weighting in your portfolio than you intended.

Do not get too worked up about this. It is good news that the better performing shares now occupy a greater place in your holdings. Do not feel the need to calculate the weightings on a daily basis and it is not a sin if you never make this calculation.

However, it can be good discipline from time to time to set out your list of holdings and assess the relative weightings. You may feel that some readjustment is required to balance out risk. This calculation is particularly useful if you are considering adding to your holdings and could help you to decide which shares to buy.

Weighting calculation

To calculate the various weightings in your portfolio, multiply the number of shares held in each company by the current share price and add together the totals. Then take each individual value, divide by the total for your portfolio and multiply by 100. This will give you the percentage holding for each company.

Here is an example of a portfolio of four shares on a specific day:

Company	Sector	No of shares	Share price	Total value	% holding
National Grid	Electricity	2,100	567p	£11,907	28.1
Royal Dutch Shell	Oil	600	1919p	£11,514	27.2
Severfield Rowan	Engineering	5,000	258p	£12,900	30.4
Taylor Wimpey	Housebuilding	25,000	24.3p	£6075	14.3
Total				£42,396	100

Equal stakes of £10,000 were originally invested in these four companies but in the meantime the stake in National Grid was increased in a rights issue and Taylor Wimpey shares fell by 40%. The holder was left to decide whether to cash in some profits in Severfield, the best performer, and to top up Taylor Wimpey to rebalance the portfolio. Alternatively, Taylor Wimpey could be ditched in favour of a better prospect.

Do not try to match the weightings of sectors on the stock exchange because:

- you cannot hope to have a holding in every single sector

- weightings change day by day as share prices go up and down. Trying to match the changes will leave you playing catch up

- the weightings of companies on the LSE are unlikely to match your personal requirements

- if you match the sector weighting of the index too closely you may find your portfolio's performance tracking that of the index – in which case you may as well simply buy a tracker fund.

Over and under weight

Incidentally, when an analyst advises being *overweight* in a stock or sector it means holding more shares than your average investment; being *underweight* correspondingly means having a smaller holding.

Fund managers give greater attention to the weightings in their portfolio than most private investors. They will periodically publish tables showing weightings by sector and by company.

It is worth looking at these occasionally for investment ideas and to see what is in favour with professional investors. Reports are available on the Association of Investment Companies website (**www.theaic.com**).

By way of illustration, the following table shows the investments of the City of London Investment Trust on 30th April 2010 as published by the trust. This trust invests purely in UK stocks, looking for income and capital growth, and its top ten holdings constituted 45.8% of the portfolio.

Table 3.2: City of London Investment Trust top 10 sectors

Sector	% of portfolio
Consumer Goods	17.0%
Financials	14.8%
Oil and Gas	13.2%
Consumer Services	12.5%
Industrials	11.0%
Utilities	9.1%
Healthcare	8.4%
Telecommunications	7.2%
Basic Materials	6.1%
Technology	0.7%

Table 3.3: City of London Investment Trust top 10 stocks

Company	% of portfolio
Royal Dutch Shell	6.4%
BP	5.9%
British American Tobacco	5.8%
GlaxoSmithKline	5.0%
Vodafone	5.0%
Diageo	4.9%
HSBC	4.4%
Tesco	2.9%
AstraZeneca	2.8%
Scottish & Southern	2.7%

Lessons learnt

- Work out how much money you can afford to invest and when it will be available

- If you have to spread your share purchases, invest in the best prospects first

- Make your portfolio as balanced as possible as soon as possible

- Be flexible and consider any company you had previously disregarded if it shows signs of improvement.

We can now consider techniques for selecting stocks.

Chapter 4.
Top Down and Bottom Up

If you read about the exploits and pronouncements of fund managers you will inevitably at some point come across those who prefer a *top down* approach and those who opt for *bottom up*.

This is a reference to the scientific way in which they select shares. Private investors may also choose to take a top down or bottom up approach, rather than simply select companies they just happen to take a fancy to.

There is no overriding need to have a methodology in choosing shares. If hit and miss – or even sticking a pin into the FT share prices page – works well for you, that's fine. However, a more structured approach to share buying ought to improve your performance.

Top down

With *top down*, you start with the general and work down to the specific.

So if the world is your oyster, you decide which continent offers the best prospects, then you narrow the search down to a country.

For example, you may consider that the exciting growth in the Pacific region is more enticing than the more mature economies in Europe and North America or the less stable environment of Latin America and Africa.

Then you need to choose a country. Perhaps you feel that Japan is stagnating, and that the former Asian tigers such as South Korea and Singapore are past their big growth phase. You are a bit worried about how open the Chinese economy is but feel that India offers equally exciting prospects.

Now you must decide which part of the Indian economy is most appealing. You are aware that many UK jobs, particularly in call centres, have been outsourced to India. Thus you decide that telecoms is where it's at and the final piece of the jigsaw is to study the Indian telecoms companies and assess each for profitability and growth.

This is very much a studied approach, demanding time and effort in carrying out careful research. While a City professional has scope to while away the hours in such amusement, ordinary investors with day jobs to attend to may find the activity rather excessive.

Nonetheless, it can be a useful discipline, especially if we are looking purely at UK stocks. In which case the order for study would be:

1. sector
2. sub-sector
3. company.

We can consider which sectors offer best prospects by considering factors such as:

- the current state of the UK and global economies
- which sectors have already factored in better prospects
- which activities offer scope for consolidation through takeovers.

Choosing a sector

Say, for example, we believe that the UK economy will recover steadily and that this will inevitably mean more construction work. Within the construction sector we must decide where spending will be concentrated.

Will the Government lead the way? If so, then will spending be on schools, hospitals and roads? Will the utilities invest in improving infrastructure, providing work for its suppliers? Will the housing market recover spectacularly as pent up supply coincides with builders completing few houses? Will construction companies be rushing to hire equipment?

Having selected the sub-sector, you can now look at individual companies.

So if you chose housebuilders, for example, you would be studying the fundamentals and share charts of the likes of Barratt Development, Persimmon and Taylor Woodrow.

Note: this is a purely hypothetical choice to illustrate the point and not a recommendation to buy housebuilders!

Having selected construction as an attractive sector, you might consider picking interesting companies in other construction sub-sectors while you are at it. You might even feel unable to choose between two or more housebuilders.

Herein lies the potential disadvantage of top down share selection. Your research has led you down one specific path and you are tempted to invest in several companies with similar characteristics.

This is fine if you get it right but supposing, using our illustrative example of selecting the construction sector, you find that the government slashes spending and tightens up on credit. Interest rates rise, investment grinds to a halt and homebuyers struggle to obtain mortgages. All your selections go down at the same time and dividends are scrapped or reduced.

Identifying sectors

One advantage of top down selection is that you can identify and discard whole sectors that offer poor prospects. For instance, anyone who has followed football would have steered well clear of football clubs as they ran up debts with very uncertain prospects of reaping the rewards of continuous top flight football.

Similarly the well documented travails of the banks during the credit crunch would have warned savvy investors out of financials, especially lenders to sub-prime borrowers.

Sometimes all companies in a sector do well or badly. For example, as the UK economy continued its long boom through to the mid 2000s it was sensible to have a car dealer in your portfolio.

Companies such as Pendragon and Lookers saw their shares soar as they expanded their franchises. Those performing less well – and some such as Reg Vardy that produced perfectly good profits – were snapped up in takeovers that offered ample returns for all investors in the sector.

Similarly when the credit crunch started to bite and consumers and fleet operators postponed new car purchases for as long as possible, it was time to get out of the entire sector.

A top down strategy helps you to identify those sectors where you may wish to have more than one share in your portfolio because the overall prospects are so promising or where you should not touch anything with a bargepole.

Differences within a sector

Where one company in a sector is doing particularly well it is tempting to assume that others in the sector must be performing likewise. This may not be so for these reasons:

- The better performing company may be taking market share from rivals

- It may have a niche market that is performing better than the general sector

- It may have secured contracts that are thus denied to rivals

- It may have better or more popular products

- It may have overseas markets that are improving better than the UK market.

Clearly the converse happens: just because one company is doing badly it does not mean that the whole barrel is rotten. We may find that the poor performer is losing market share or has lost contracts while others are picking up more business.

One advantage of top down investing is that it reminds you to distinguish that there are often winners and losers in a given sector.

Equally important is that it helps you to sift the better prospects from their weaker brethren. Because one supermarket is reporting higher sales, it does not mean that they are all on the up.

Tesco became the UK's number one by taking sales from its rivals, particularly from Sainsbury, in the days when the former top dog was in long term decline. The recovery at Sainsbury was helped by problems at Morrison when the Bradford-based chains with nationwide ambitions bit off more than it could chew in its takeover of Safeway.

If Procter & Gamble sells more soap powder it does not necessarily mean that we are all getting cleaner. It could be that sales have been gained from Unilever.

Example: milk shake-up

A stark and highly public example came when UK supermarkets 'rationalised' their milk supply contracts, which meant they decided to source supplies from one or two rather than three or four dairies. This was possible as Robert Wiseman Dairies, Dairy Crest and Arla Foods had all built nationwide networks. Milk supply contracts, typically lasting several years, were coming up for renewal.

This was the sequence of events, the values shown representing the annual contracts:

- **May 2004:** Asda switches £70 million from Wiseman and £20 million from Dairy Crest to Arla.

- **August 2004:** Sainsbury switches £66 million from Arla to Wiseman.

- **August 2004:** Tesco switches £60 million from Dairy Crest to Wiseman.

- **May 2005**: Morrison switches £40 million from Wiseman, £30 million to Dairy Crest and £10 million to Arla.

The sum total of the market is the same. It is just that, as the dust settles, we find Robert Wiseman selling £16 million worth of extra milk, Dairy Crest a net £50 million less and Arla on balance £34 million more.

Naturally, movements in the respective share prices reflected the comings and goings of the supermarket contracts.

Bottom up

With this method of stock picking we take an 'innocent until proven guilty' approach to individual companies. We take a fancy to a company, then check if there is anything in the wider scheme of things to persuade us we are wrong.

This time the order goes:

1. company

2. sub sector

3. sector

4. UK economy

5. world economy.

At each stage working upwards we are checking whether there are any reasons why the company we fancy may not live up to our expectations.

Case study: Sage

Most UK investors will have heard of Sage, a software supplier that bounced to prominence in the tech boom at the end of the last millennium. Unlike many of its contemporaries, Sage also gained fame for surviving as other former stock market darlings fell by the wayside.

Sage has been a frequent subject of assessments in the tips columns of national newspapers and it is covered by a wide range of analysts.

So is it worth an investment?

Website

Our first port of call is the Sage website for a bit of basic information. We can see that it is based in Newcastle-upon-Tyne, where it was founded in 1981, and that it has grown into a worldwide company since taking a UK stock market listing in 1989.

Initially Sage made its name supplying accounting software for small businesses, something it still does, but it has expanded to provide a wider range of products including software to manage finances, run the payroll, manage customer and supplier relationships, plan the business and support human resources.

Sage has more than 750,000 small and medium sized customers in the UK alone but it has expanded in the United States and in Europe. It now has more than 6 million customers worldwide and employs nearly 15,000 people.

It also maintains and updates the software and runs training courses, so there is follow-up revenue after the initial sales.

For most of its first 20 years it had one chief executive, Paul Walker, which gave continuity and a clear sense of direction.

It all sounds pretty dynamic, but then you would expect a company's own website to put a decent gloss on the performance. Naturally we also want to study the fundamentals of the company before we look at the wider picture. We have to be satisfied on the merits of the company before we waste time trawling through the entire sector.

The numbers

Turnover has risen consistently since the turn of the century, with overseas sales growing faster than UK sales. Profits have also risen steadily on every basis: Ebitda, operating, pre-tax and earnings per share. All these figures are forecast to continue growing.

Likewise the dividend has increased steadily. Dividend cover has generally been quite conservative, especially in the early years of the 2000s when cash was conserved to develop the business.

The sector

On the whole, the business looks sound and promising, so what of the subsector, supplying software for small businesses?

Small businesses suffered heavily in the recession as they were squeezed by bigger, more powerful players who could cut selling prices to maintain volumes and delay paying for goods and services from small suppliers.

They also suffer disproportionately from red tape as it is expensive to support a human resources or health and safety expert to cater for a handful of employees.

However, the small business sector has continued to thrive against the odds: the Federation of Small Businesses has well over 200,000 members and the number has grown steadily since the FSB was set up in 1974.

These businesses on the whole do not have the in-house expertise to devise and develop their own computer systems but neither do they have the cash to splash out on expensive software. They need software that is designed for smaller business and adapted for their own specific needs.

Small companies that can not afford a separate finance director still need to keep accounts. If a computer can do the job, all you need is someone inputting in the data. Yes, it has to be someone competent and trustworthy but not necessarily someone commanding a premium salary.

Thus there is a substantial potential market for Sage, not only here but in the US and Europe.

There is admittedly an element of risk in being heavily dependent on one very specific market, but Sage benefits from a distinct absence of direct competition in the UK, where several software companies are content with their own niches. Thus, Alterian and Autonomy specialise in managing web content, Aveva concentrates on energy and shipbuilding software and Micro Focus sets its sights on improving its clients' existing computer systems.

There is a more clearly developed subsector for small business software in the United States but even there we see few direct competitors and enough business to go round. Sage has 21% of the market, Microsoft 12%, Oracle 9%, Intuit 6% and SAP 3%.

What, then, of the wider computer software sector, which has enjoyed a short but spectacular life so far?

There is no point in dwelling forever over the excesses of the late 1990s, the grossly overpriced shares, the companies with no income, the products with no market …

A handful of companies, such as Sage, that were in their infancy then have emerged all the stronger after seeing less well run rivals fall by the wayside. Others have emerged since with genuine business plans. These companies are succeeding because, like Sage, they have:

- a real product and real income
- niche markets that were not catered for by other companies
- products that meet a real need
- programmes to develop and improve products to meet the needs of customers better
- the ability to diversify into related products
- projects to expand into overseas markets without overstretching themselves
- dominant positions that make it hard for rivals to muscle in
- a strong after sales service that means revenue comes in even during dips in sales.

One could arguably move up one further stage and include the whole computer sector with hardware, components, peripherals and even mobile telephony. This is a growing sector that is increasingly pervading every aspect of our lives, thus providing continued expansion.

If we feel that this is a fair analysis then there are no obvious factors in the wider world to deter us from our original intent. It would, however, do no harm just to go back and check whether we are still happy with the company itself and whether now is a good time to invest or hold off for a better opportunity.

Figure 4.1: Sage

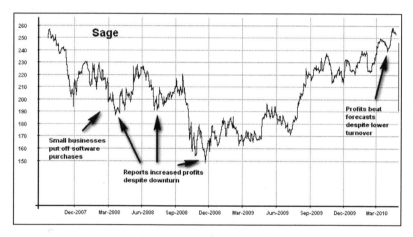

Sage did go through a difficult time in 2007 and 2008, when small businesses delayed investing in new software or upgrades during the economic uncertainty, when cash was tight and bank loans were hard to come by.

The company reacted quickly by reducing its own headcount by 1000, thus cutting costs in line with income. In due course Sage started to sign up new customers while existing clients were beginning to upgrade their technology.

Sage shares can be quite erratic but that does mean there are buying opportunities from time to time. They tend to anticipate rather than follow stock market trends so it can pay to get in – or out – before the market turns.

Best of both worlds

There is no reason why you should not combine top down and bottom up methods of stock picking As with everything in stock market investing, it is better to be flexible than hidebound.

So if a particular stock comes to your attention or is recommended in your newspaper's tips column you can the start from the bottom up. However, if nothing springs to mind and you have cash to invest, start with the wider picture and see where working downwards leads you.

Chapter 5.
Fundamentals

Having decided how much to invest and when, we can move smoothly on to the question of how we actually select the stocks. What criteria can we use to determine our selections?

Fundamental data is our key tool in deciding whether a company's shares are good value.

By *fundamental data* we mean figures based on a company's earnings, dividends and share price. These can refer either to past data as issued in the latest annual figures or future data based on forecasts by analysts.

Both sets of data have their uses and drawbacks.

Historic figures are reliable because they represent what actually happened. It is particularly informative to look on a company's website and trace the figures over the past five years to see what progress if any has been maintained. However, historic figures are out of date even by the time they are issued and may give little clue to what will happen in the current financial year, which has far more influence on the share price.

Future or prospective figures, based on analysts' forecasts, are a more reliable guide to the future, but they are only opinions, not facts, and analysts can be wide of the mark. Also prospective figures are of little value if only one or two analysts cover a particular company. We need a consensus of several analysts' predictions for a more accurate view.

The figures will tend to move day by day as share prices move, since the share price forms part of the calculation for the yield and the price/earnings ratio. The difference between historic and future data is more pronounced in the case of P/E ratios, since earnings tend to fluctuate much more from year to year than dividends.

If you check the data in the share price columns in a daily newspaper, be warned that the *Daily Telegraph* uses historic data and the *Financial Times*, the *Times* and the *Independent* use forecasts.

What to look for

We are looking for companies with high yields and low P/E ratios.

A high yield means that we expect to get a larger dividend payout: a yield of 10% suggests £10 of income from every £100 invested whereas a 5% yields indicates we will receive only half as much.

With P/E ratios, a low figure implies that the company has high earnings for its share price, while a high figure suggests that the company is overvalued.

There could be a good reason for a company looking cheap. It may be that investors fear it will not live up to expectations, and perhaps analysts are considering downgrading their forecasts. On the other hand, it could mean that the company really is cheap and we have spotted a bargain.

Similarly, a highly rated company may be sought after because it has a reputation for fulfilling high expectations or it may mean that the shares are too expensive. We must do our research, looking at the company's performance and outlook, and make our own decision.

Within any particular sector we would expect to see some convergence of yields and P/E ratios as the various companies face similar opportunities and challenges. However, even within a sector we may see a wide range of yields and price/earnings ratios, often with some shares near their year's high while others have languished around their lowest level for the past 12 months.

There are various possible reasons for this discrepancy.

- The sector may contain companies with disparate activities

- Some companies will be perceived as better run than others

- Some companies will have performed better over the past year or two and the market believes this outperformance will continue

- There may be a change of leadership in a company that is seen in a positive or negative light.

Company analysis

Let us take a selection of companies in the electricals sector and consider the differences in their fundamentals on a specific day. One point to note is that P/Es in this sector are substantially higher than the market average – which at the time was in the low teens. We should be asking ourselves why this sector looks expensive and whether we feel that the premium rating is justified.

Company	Shares	Year high	Year low	Yield	P/E
Chloride	286p	302p	133p	1.8%	32.4
Dialight	310p	310p	213.25p	2.1%	17.7
Invensys	272.5p	349p	213.25p	1.1%	15.3
Laird	115.5p	223p	106.5p	5.5%	--
Morgan Crucible	178p	219p	81.5p	3.9%	25.3
TT Electronic	107.25p	109.5p	26p	--	--
XP Power	582p	602p	202.25p	2.9%	18.1

Source: *Daily Telegraph*, 5 June 2010

One of the first things we notice in the table is that Chloride, a supplier of high-tech electricity supply systems for clients such as HSBC and Sainsbury, has a much higher price/earnings ratio than the others. Its shares have more than doubled from its low point of the past year to stand near their recent high point.

The yield is admittedly not the lowest but the sector mostly offers better prospects.

Why would Chloride shares be so expensive?

A little research soon gives us the answer. Chloride is the subject of a takeover bid. It was approached two months previously by American power giant Emerson Electric with a £732 million bid.

Figure 5.1: Chloride

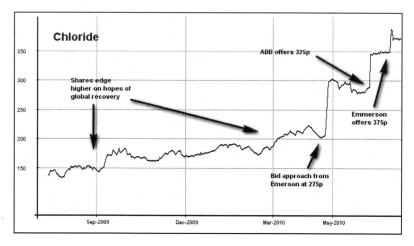

Although the Chloride board had rejected the offer of 275p a share as undervaluing the company, Emerson held talks with Chloride's major investors to discuss the possibility of launching a hostile bid. The Americans were expected to return to the negotiating table with an offer of 300p a share.

We can see now why Chloride is so highly priced. We can also see that it may offer little scope for buying in at this stage, certainly for investors looking for income. If the bid goes through then we have only a small, short term capital gain.

If the bid fails then the shares will fall back, offering a better buying opportunity at a company that was doing well anyway. Results a month earlier had shown profits down 6% but sales were up 3% and markets were recovering, with the order book at a record level.

As it turned out, Swiss power and industrial automation company ABB suddenly popped up with an offer of 325p a share, only for Emerson to return with 375p, which was agreed with the Chloride board. It goes to show that if you are already a shareholder in a company that receives a takeover bid it is usually best to hang on in hope, though for a capital gain rather than income.

Laird

Laird, in contrast, stands near its low point for the year and well down from its recent high. It designs, manufactures and supplies products and services to the electronics industry, particularly critical components for wireless applications.

Its yield is a very tempting 5.5% but the table gives no P/E ratio. We should find out whether this is an omission on the part of the newspaper or if there is a reason for the gap. Financial website Hemscott was showing a P/E of about nine times earnings at this stage compared with a sector average of 15 and a market average of 12.

Laird's most recent financial figures give grounds for concern. In the calendar year 2009 it saw turnover fall from £635.3 million to £528.8 million while pre-tax profits slumped from £26.5 million to only £4.6 million. Basic earnings per share from continuing operations gave a negative figure, hence the omission[2] of a P/E in the Daily Telegraph table which is based on historic figures. The Hemscott calculations are based on analysts' forecasts for the current year.

The total dividend was reduced from 10.31p in 2008 to 6.84p. All these financial figures could be found on the Laird website.

Laird had suffered badly in the recession, with its share price falling from 550p in September 2007 to a low of 50p in March 2009; and a recovery to around 180p in the summer of 2009 has petered out.

---

[2] P/E ratios are not calculated if earnings are negative.

Figure 5.2: Laird

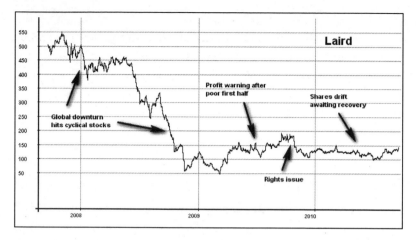

This is clearly a cyclical stock, depending heavily on how the economy is perceived to be doing. The shares peaked fractionally after the FTSE 100 did and hit the bottom at around the same time. The recovery petered out in the autumn of 2009. Laird shares have badly underperformed the market and the sector since the middle of 2008.

So what has gone wrong?

As chief executive Peter Hill said when he revealed these figures in March 2010, trading conditions had been extremely difficult during the previous year. The question for investors is whether Laird has prospects for recovery. If so, that yield could be very attractive.

Remember that boards are extremely reluctant to cut the dividend twice so a further reduction in the payout is unlikely. If the dividend was going to be scrapped, that would have happened in 2009.

Signs of recovery

Hill said that by the end of 2009 Laird had seen some recovery in a number of markets and this, together with the cost cutting undertaken as markets fell away, led to a significant improvement in underlying profits and operating margins in the second half of 2009.

He added:

> "While the profile of an economic recovery remains uncertain, we have so far in 2010 seen a continuation of the trends experienced in the second half of 2009."

Hill also pointed to a strong inward cash flow and a quick check of the balance sheet shows net debt down from £139.5 million at the end of 2008 to £45.4 million a year later, giving the group much better prospects of recovery.

An interim management statement issued on 27th April claimed that most of Laird's markets were showing a progressive recovery from the depressed conditions of 2009 and, as expected, Laird produced underlying profit before tax ahead of the corresponding period in the previous year, with the better trends seen in the second half of 2009 continuing.

Growth was strongest in the divisions with higher profit margins, which is further good news. Combined with cost cutting during the downturn, it means margins will be higher overall.

Hill pointed to increased demand for Laird's products across the key markets of IT, telecom and datacom and the consumer electronics markets, where he believed that Laird was growing revenue faster than the underlying market growth after winning new customers and the introducing new products.

Reasons to consider investing

We may conclude from our analysis that Laird is a potential candidate for inclusion in our portfolio, irrespective of whether we are looking for income or growth. It does look as if the market has punished Laird for its disappointing performance in 2009 and not fully factored in the prospects for improvement in 2010.

Admittedly there is good cause to worry over whether recovery will continue, given the crisis still being played out in the Eurozone, where Greece, Spain and Portugal were forced into deflationary measures to curb their government debt problems. These are additional factors we must take into account.

However, if Laird does continue to make progress then the dividend will be maintained and the share price will rise. We should take comfort from the decision of stockbroker UBS to raise its rating on Laird from *neutral* to *buy* at the end of May.

Please note that this is a snapshot of Laird at a particular moment in time, 5th June 2010. Circumstances will change as time moves on and the share price could be considerably different at a later stage.

TT Electronics

What are we to make, then, of TT Electronics, which designs and makes electronic and electrical components for the defence, aerospace, medical, automotive and other industrial electronics markets?

It sounds as if it is in a similar situation to Laird, and indeed there are blanks in both the yield and P/E columns, which looks ominous. Yet TT is trading near its 12-month high at four times the level it sunk to. We should be asking ourselves why TT shares have recovered as far as they have and whether there are prospects for more upside.

Figure 5.3: TT

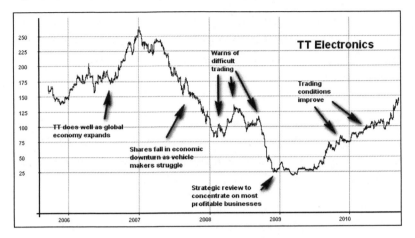

The share chart shows that it was pretty much downhill all the way for TT from the end of 2006, when it was priced at over 250p, to the first quarter of 2009, so there is still some way to go to return to past glory.

TT warned in March 2008 that it was taking a 'cautious view for the current year' given the difficulties in credit markets. And it reiterated the message in August that year when it reported lower first half profits and warned that trading conditions in the second half were proving difficult.

Despite this commendable frankness, TT had to issue a profits warning in October 2008 when it became clear that full year profits would fall short of analysts' expectations.

As revenue deteriorated rapidly in the final quarter of the year, TT acted to restructure the group to concentrate on the most profitable markets but that was too late to prevent a near halving of pre-tax profits to £17.3 million for 2008. Oddly enough, the announcement of the poor figures, accompanied by a warning that 'market conditions have become even more challenging, with less visibility of market demand', coincided with the bottom of the market for the shares.

The importance of strategic reviews

A great deal was riding on the outcome of the strategic review, which identified the need to cut costs and to concentrate on the most profitable markets. It is, incidentally, remarkable how many companies suddenly stumble on what one might feel ought to be the policy anyway.

Investors may have been comforted by news that the restructuring programme was being accelerated, or that cash was still being generated and the balance sheet remained strong, but it was still a brave move to buy at this stage since trading conditions remained 'testing'.

TT's largest market sector is in supplying equipment, mainly sensors, to vehicle makers. This exposed the group to the sharp decline in the production of new vehicles during the credit crunch and at that stage it seemed possible that one of the larger US manufacturers would seek protection from its creditors. In this event, the group might not recover all the money owed to it.

TT produced a pre-tax loss in the first half of 2009 and, although trading picked up later in the year, it was still in the red at the pre-tax level for the full year after exceptional charges from the restructuring. Since TT had indicated a year earlier that it would not pay a dividend unless it was covered at least twice by earnings there was no payout.

Thus we can see why the table is unable to give up a yield or a P/E ratio. The latest figures showed no profit and no dividend.

Weighing up the pros and cons

The good news when these figures were released in March 2010 was that the improved trading conditions seen at the end of 2009 had continued into 2010 and there was greater visibility of earnings in some markets. Trading was at that point slightly ahead of expectations.

Also on the positive side was a halving of net debt to £56.9 million.

However, much of the improvement had come from the car scrappage scheme operated in several countries including the UK, US and Germany in an attempt to stimulate consumer demand during the credit crunch. These schemes were drawing to a close.

Also there was an artificial boost from customers rebuilding stock levels that had been reduced aggressively in late 2008 and 2009. While this boost is welcome it will inevitably run its course.

TT is a well run company with quality products and it has tried to diversify away from the cyclical car industry, winning several contracts with the US Defense Department for instance. However, it is still at the mercy of the global economy.

Clearly there is little attraction here for income seekers until profits have been rebuilt to allow the payment of a dividend, which may take quite some time. The position for those wanting capital gains is somewhat obscure.

The best chance for buying has clearly been missed and the issue now is whether TT can keep up the momentum given the uncertainties over the scale of the economic recovery.

Let us look briefly at the other companies in the list.

Dialight

Dialight specialises in LED lights for factories, signs and traffic lights. Having fallen from a peak of 250p at the end of 2006 its shares bottomed rather earlier than the rest of the UK stock market at 100p late in 2008.

Figure 5.4: Dialight

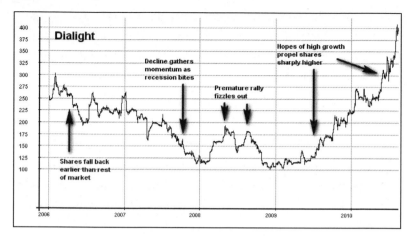

Results for 2009 showed profits down 6% from £5.64 million to £5.28 million on almost unchanged revenue as better sales in the second half offset a weak first half.

A yield of 2.1% makes the shares reasonably attractive to income investors but not overwhelmingly so, while the P/E is above average for the market as a whole but not for the sector as investors factored in continued growth.

Dialight's prognosis, repeated in May 2010, was that the group was in the early stages of a period of high growth as LED technology was increasingly adopted in lighting. If you believe that is a fair assessment then the shares look decent value at this stage.

XP Power

XP Power's fundamental data shows a similar picture. While the shares are a little below the year's high they are nearly treble the bottom of the market price. The yield is higher than that for Dialight, giving an attractive appearance for dividend seekers, while the P/E is a little higher so the shares are starting to get off the radar for growth specialists.

Shares in XP Power, a supplier of critical power control components for the electronics industry, lost three-quarters of their value in crashing from 525p in March 2007 to well below 150p in early 2009, but they more than made up for that by zooming north of 600p at the start of 2010.

Figure 5.5: XP

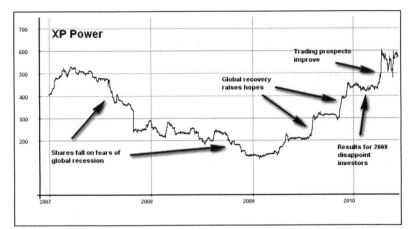

This recovery suggests that the best chance for capital gains has gone and, indeed, the shares have come off the boil as highly satisfied punters took the profits.

Full year results for the 2009 calendar year were a little disappointing with profits and turnover both lower. This announcement in February 2010 did the share price no good but the company said current trading was encouraging, with most markets recovering. The dividend total was raised from 21p to 22p as a signal of confidence after no change in the interim payment.

Invensys

Software and computer services group Invensys has seen its shares move more erratically. They kept rising along with the market until the middle of 2007, turning back later than most cyclical stocks but nonetheless crashing from 430p to 200p in a comparatively short time frame.

An upward surge to 350p in the first half of 2008, against a background of a falling stock market, was impressive but short lived and the shares were down to 120p by November that year. Another strong burst then took them to 350p in March 2010 before another decline set in.

Figure 5.6: Invensys

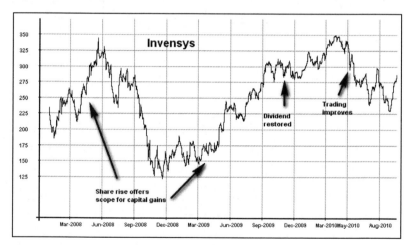

The share price chart shows that there is ample ammunition for capital gains, with the shares swinging about more than most – provided you get your timing right. The yield of 1.1% is not going to lure in the income investors, though, especially as the downturn in the share price suggests there may be better chances to buy in.

Invensys has a financial year running to the end of March. In the first half to September 2009 it reported a fall in orders, revenue and operating profit. However, it did restore the dividend as a sign of confidence despite admitting that the economic climate was still adverse. The best it could offer was that 'we are beginning to see some early signs of stabilisation and possible modest recovery'.

Progress in the second half was foreseen, with parts of the operation gaining market share. Sure enough, the full year results released in May 2010 showed better figures all round with a higher order book and no debt.

Morgan Crucible

Morgan Crucible specialises in carbon and ceramic components for industrial use. Its shares held up much longer than most, almost to the end of 2007, before plunging from 325p to 175p in pretty short order. A recovery in mid-2008 was not sustained and before the year was out they were down to 75p.

Figure 5.7: Morgan Crucible

The recovery since then has been spasmodic, with the shares failing to reach 2008 highs. Even at the point we have selected for our analysis they are off the top though they are more than double their recent low.

The yield at 3.9% is very attractive although the P/E of 25.3 suggests that the shares are fully valued, and broker Goldman Sachs cut its rating on the shares from buy to neutral just a few days later.

Full year results to 3rd January 2010 showed revenue up 13% but alas pre-tax profits slumped from £82.8 million to £31.4 million, a figure that the company chose not to highlight in its statement.

A trading update in April was more encouraging, saying that the company was optimistic for the rest of 2010 after trading conditions continued to improve in the first quarter, driven by robust demand from Asia and improving markets in North America.

Operating profit and margins were above the same period a year earlier and were in line with management expectations as the business benefited from the cost cuts it made in the previous year.

Morgan Crucible said market conditions had improved for its thermal ceramics division, with increasing revenue from India and China offsetting a slower European market. The majority of the technical ceramics division's markets had also improved and order books rose in the first quarter, especially in North America, although there had been some weakness in the medical device markets because of destocking.

The company said it expected further improvement in the second half.

It is always very useful, when a company is claiming that things are getting better, if it specifies which areas are improving and where there is any lingering cause for concern. You can feel much more confident investing in a company if you have a clearer picture.

Lessons learnt

- Companies issue, on a regular basis, information that helps us to decide whether they are worthwhile investments

- A high yield and a low price/earnings ratio suggest that a company is cheap but find out whether there is good reason for investors to shun the shares

- Within each sector there is likely to be a wide range of yields and P/Es

- Historic data covers what actually happened but is out of date; prospective data refers to forecasts of what is expected in the current financial year and the subsequent year.

Chapter 6.
Choosing Between Cyclicals and Defensives

Having determined what factors we are looking for in a company, we can move on to consider what type of company we are looking at and how it fits into the economic cycle.

You will often see companies referred to as being either cyclical or defensive. An explanation:

- *Cyclicals* are the companies whose fortunes ride up and down in line with the economy, increasing their profits and dividends in the good times but suffering in the downturns. They are called cyclicals because they follow the economic cycle.

- *Defensives* are companies that sell pretty much the same amount of goods and services whatever the state of the economy. They do not enjoy the boom times as cyclical stocks do but neither are they set back so badly in tougher times. They are referred to as defensive stocks because they are seen as a line of defence when your portfolio is under attack from falling share prices.

The theory is that you should buy cyclical stocks when the stock market is rising and dump them in favour of defensive stocks when the stock market is falling.

That is the theory.

Like all stock market theories it has some truth in it and like all stock market theories it should not be followed slavishly.

The following chart shows the relative performance of the construction and healthcare sectors. While the market was rising strongly between 2004 and 2007 construction stocks were obviously the ones to be in; but when the market started falling a switch into the defensive healthcare sector would have resulted in fewer losses than seen in the construction sector. Elsewhere, we can see that the performance of these two sectors diverges over many periods.

Figure 6.1: Construction sector v Healthcare sector (2004–2010)

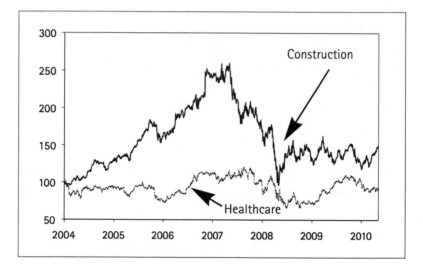

When markets move in a particular direction, up or down, the overwhelming majority of shares move in the same direction. Do not assume that because you have bought defensive stocks you are somehow immune to falls in share prices. Do not assume that all cyclical stocks will rise as the good times roll. Some are better managed than others.

The other side of the coin is that well run companies that react quickly to changing circumstances should outperform the market whatever the economic cycle is telling us.

Timing issues

You may feel that if you are investing for the long term it does not matter too much whether a stock is cyclical or defensive, since you will be riding through the cycle and it will all come out in the wash.

It could, even so, affect the timing of your buys. Investing in cyclical stocks at the bottom rather than the top of the market obviously makes more sense but you should err towards defensives if the market is looking iffy.

In any case, the market takes some note of whether setbacks are temporary. Cyclical stocks do not suddenly collapse. There is a time lag during which potential sellers hold back, either because they hope for early economic recovery or because they are slow to react.

After all, the market is used to the ups and downs of trading life. Investors do not buy shares in chocolates maker Thorntons around St Valentine's Day or Christmas when sales rise and dump them in summer when chocolates melt. The market takes a longer view on how sales are moving over the year as a whole.

Predictable cycles

Some cycles are entirely predictable. We know, for instance, that the football World Cup comes round every four years. As long as at least one of the four home nations reaches the finals then sales by sports retailers will rise for a couple of months leading up to the event.

Other events such as the Rugby Union World Cup, the Ashes cricket series and the Olympic Games may also boost sports sales.

Television broadcasters also rake it in at big sporting events, depending on who has the TV rights. For instance ITV, which split the 2010 football World Cup matches with the BBC and broadcast England's first match in prime time, saw bookings for the main ITV channel soar 30% in June 2010 compared with June 2009. Takings for the month topped £100 million, as they did four years earlier.

This kind of cyclical boost should always be seen in context. One great month does not compensate for the other 47 months in a four-year cycle. ITV had been increasingly squeezed by rival broadcasters, mainly BSkyB, and advertising rates had fallen so ITV was running to stand still in terms of income.

The age of digital broadcasting has brought a proliferation of television channels, and ITV had to keep pace, launching ITV2, ITV3 and ITV4. This spread the advertising icing more thinly on the cake while costs were rising.

Figure 6.2: ITV

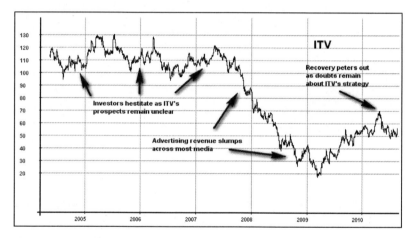

It is only one stage further on in the thought process to realise that shares in a cyclical company are not dumped at the first sign of bad news. The slide will gather momentum only when it becomes clear that the downturn is either more severe than previously thought or shows signs of lasting longer than earlier expectations.

We can see at ITV that it was possible to get out at 100p or more for much of the second half of 2007, long after the first cracks in the global financial system started to appear. Indeed, those shareholders who, quite reasonably, failed to see the extent of the economic crisis as the floodgates opened around August probably felt justified in holding on when the shares enjoyed a temporary blip and even at year end it was not too late to cut losses.

It was almost two years after the slide started before ITV shares hit the bottom.

When the bubble in technology stocks burst the shares did not collapse overnight. It took fully three years to weed out companies with little sustainable revenue. The stock market was reluctant to believe that the boom was over.

Visibility of earnings

Some companies have what is referred to as good *visibility of earnings*. That means you can see where the income is coming from for months or, preferably, years ahead.

A defensive company will tend to have good visibility of earnings. You know that contracts have been signed to provide work over a period of time so the income is guaranteed (provided the client does not go bust). Where those contracts are for government and local authority schemes you can be pretty sure that they will be honoured, or at least compensation will be paid.

For instance, a contract to build a school will provide work for a building company for several months; a contract to maintain the school will provide work for several years.

Other companies live more hand to mouth. Generally speaking they sell to the general public whose spending patterns are more susceptible to economic change. In particular, the purchase of items that we can manage without will be postponed indefinitely and possibly even be cancelled.

We can manage without the latest mobile phone so we can postpone buying one until better times. If we delay long enough we can actually skip one generation and buy the next update, so the intervening purchase we would have made when cash was plentiful is lost forever.

This is indeed what happened when the tech bubble burst in 2000: sales that tech companies claimed had been merely postponed into the next financial year in fact never happened. Companies simply abandoned upgrades to their systems for three years.

Similarly we could decide not to renew our car after three years as we normally do and hang on for four years. If our finances have not improved we will soon find that six years have passed and we have missed the intervening model altogether.

Let us now look at the two types of share in more detail.

Cyclicals

Prime examples of cyclical industries are manufacturing, the steel industry, travel and construction. These sectors produce things we can live without when money is tight and are thus the ones you will be inclined to avoid in an economic downturn.

When we decide we have to tighten our belts, we realise that we can manage without luxury handbags and world cruises. We postpone buying a new car or moving to a bigger house. We buy cheaper food and eat at Pizza Hut rather than the Savoy Grill.

Cyclical stocks are not all hit at the same time – a point worth remembering whenever the market starts to turn. Retailing is affected immediately as we reduce spending; manufacturers of the goods we decide to do without then see their orders fall; the chain runs back through distributors and warehouses to suppliers of components and raw materials; machinery makers see orders dry up.

The banks that finance economic activity are affected at every stage of the process.

Some cyclicals can react more quickly and more decisively than others by, for example, laying off staff. However, there is a limit to the action that can be taken and the main impediment is property, which is fixed and expensive. You can give sales staff a week's notice; surrendering a 25-year lease on a shop is a lot trickier, especially as the landlord will also be feeling the pinch and replacement tenants will be in short supply.

The construction industry is particularly hamstrung. It can take years from taking an option to buy land, working through the planning process, demolishing existing buildings and clearing the site, putting up the new block and welcoming the first tenants. Builders of office blocks and shopping centres can find that they are just gearing up as the market starts to turn down.

To summarise, main cyclical sectors of the economy are:

- Aerospace
- Automotive
- Banks
- Construction
- Engineering and Industrial
- Media
- Mining
- Property
- Retailing
- Travel and Leisure

Cyclical shares tend to suffer from a double whammy that exaggerates the impact of economic downturns and upswings.

In the downturn, customers hold off buying for various reasons such as hoping that recession will force down prices over the coming month. Retailers run down stocks to a minimum. Production lines grind to a trickle and staff are laid off.

So when the upturn does come there is a shortage of goods or service personnel. Consequently there is a scramble to rebuild stocks before demand pushes prices up again.

In the meantime, weaker companies have gone out of business or been taken over by stronger rivals, so there is less competition. As prices are thus driven higher, new companies expand into the market, creating the conditions for the next boom and bust.

Let us look at two sectors that are particularly at the mercy of the economic winds of change.

Industrials and engineering

Industrial and engineering stocks are firmly in the camp of the cyclicals. This sector was heavily sold in 2008 when investors feared that the global economy was going to grind to a halt. Here was a classic case of customers running stocks down for fear that construction projects and sales of finished products would dry up.

Although the industrial sector of the UK economy has dwindled over the years, from representing more than a third of GDP to only 12%, it still contains some sizeable companies including IMI, Weir, Rotork and Charter International.

In all, there are eight UK industrial and engineering companies in the 350 largest companies on the London Stock Exchange.

UK engineering companies have suffered from cheap competition from countries such as China and Mexico while British labour rates remain comparatively high. They have tried to get round the problem by importing cheap components and concentrating on higher value goods where labour costs form a smaller proportion of total costs.

These companies have also, where possible, attempted to alleviate the effects of a downturn in the UK by exporting to other regions, although that was of little comfort during the global downturn.

This sector therefore suffered more than most between mid-2007 and March 2009 as shares fell across the board. However, they also led the way upwards in the recovery during the summer of 2009.

The improvement continued into the first half of 2010 and Industrial and Engineering was the best performing sector on the UK stock market in the five months to the end of May, with the FTSE 350 Industrial and Engineering index gaining 19% while the FTSE 350 index of large and middle sized companies came off the boil, falling 3% overall in the five months and dropping back 10% from a peak in April.

Case study: IMI

Shares in the specialist engineer have shadowed the FTSE all-share index remarkably closely. A member of the FTSE 250 index of mid-sized companies, IMI makes highly specialised components with some products used in extreme conditions such as oil exploration.

During the second half of the bull market that lasted from March 2003 to August 2007 IMI generally tracked higher. Profits rose in 2005 as IMI successfully restructured its operations with a sale of non-core businesses culminating in the disposal of Polypipe.

This took the group out of low margin products and into specialist engineering products such as air conditioning, air brakes for trucks and industrial pneumatic equipment, with acquisitions augmenting strong organic growth.

Figure 6.3: IMI

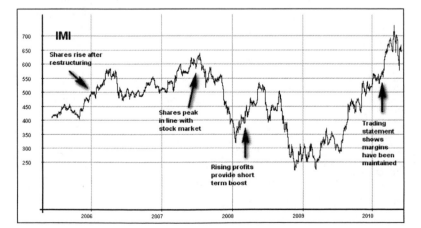

The shares did fall back quite sharply in May 2006 for no good reason. Perhaps there was an element of profit taking after the strong run or perhaps investors felt some concern when the AGM that month was told that investment would be stepped up and that bolt-on acquisitions would be sought, which meant cash would be tied up.

If that was indeed a concern, common sense soon prevailed. After a rise in profits and the dividend in 2005 it was already clear that 2006 would see even better figures. Chairman Norman Askew pointed out that some of the investment would pay to transfer more manufacturing capacity to already established low cost facilities, raising the percentage of total production in these territories from around 25% to 40% over the following three years with a consequent improvement in operating margins.

IMI shares soon resumed their upward march and they peaked at 640p in the middle of 2007, having gained more than 50% over the previous 12 months. At this point the stock market began to wake up to the sheer scale of the US sub-prime lending disaster and the potential global recession.

As a cyclical stock, IMI was particularly affected and the halving of the share price in about six months was as severe as for any stock at this time. As it happened, it was at the peak in the market that IMI discovered irregular and possibly illegal payments to a number of agents over the winning of contracts for its 'severe service' business making components for use in harsh working environments.

IMI likewise enjoyed the premature boom in share prices in the first quarter of 2008, helped by an 8% increase in profits for 2007 and a bullish outlook for 2008, before joining the resumed downward trend to March 2009.

Once again we saw IMI joining the stampede with shares running away until the end of the year, although there was a setback in summer that was peculiar to IMI in the shape of doubts over the recovery in its specific markets.

Show of confidence

IMI did edge downwards in early 2010, again in line with the market, but then shot away while other shares stuttered. Investors warmed to a trading statement in March showing that operating margins had been maintained at 13% despite 2009 being one of the worst on record for the industries that IMI supplied. As a mark of confidence, IMI reinstated its progressive dividend policy, having previously said it would do no more than maintain the dividend throughout the economic downturn.

Although revenue for the year had fallen 6%, pre-tax profits rose, also by 6%, and cash flow was strong, helping to reduce net debt by 42% to £172 million.

Just under two months later it got better. IMI reported a significant improvement in its business over the intervening seven weeks, so strong that it felt obliged to bring forward its next trading statement.

One division was showing a 25% increase in orders for the first half of 2010 thanks to a definite improvement in end markets. Analysts scrambled to upgrade profit forecasts for the year.

This was a ringing endorsement of the decision to invest through the downturn. Companies that do so should come out stronger on the other side. In this way well run cyclical companies can buck the trend to some extent.

However, it was worth bearing in mind that IMI's order book is relatively short and it was impossible to predict what would happen beyond the end of the calendar year.

Travel and leisure

One sector that suffers particularly from the double whammy effect of boom and bust is the travel sector. Hotel rooms and airline seats are block booked a year in advance as the travel companies attempt to gauge demand with very little evidence to go on apart from the previous year's bookings.

Spending on leisure and pleasure has exploded over several decades as growing numbers of people found they had the time and the money to spend outside working hours. Package holiday companies boomed, theme parks mushroomed, pubs became dining experiences and hotels expanded.

The trouble is that, in the downturns, leisure spending can be postponed or cancelled. A holiday missed this year could be compensated for by two holidays next year but by and large that does not happen. If you cannot afford to go to the Costa del Sol this year you will still be rebuilding your finances when you plan next year's break.

It is important, though, to distinguish between the various players in this field. The FTSE 300 Travel and Leisure index includes holiday companies, airlines, bus and train operators, catering companies and bookmakers. They are not all affected equally by the economic swings.

Holiday swings

Package holidays and cruises are hit first, partly because of self-inflicted wounds.

In times of uncertainty, when you may lose your job or are forced to take a pay cut, it is easy to hold off from making a booking. There will always be a chance to pick up a last minute deal if our fears prove unfounded.

This has a domino effect. Holiday companies with excess capacity start to panic and reduce prices, possibly even selling holidays at a loss. Better to get what income they can given their commitment to hotels and airlines to take space whether it is filled or not.

Holidaymakers then hold off in the hope of securing last minute bargains, thus exacerbating the situation.

Next year the holiday companies book less space, thus passing the effects of the downturn onto hotels and airlines. However, when the upturn comes the holiday companies find they are able to push up prices because of the lost capacity. Since the hotels are suffering, the rooms can be secured at a cheaper rate so the holiday companies win twice over.

Transport shuttle

Airlines, along with rail and bus companies, are not affected quite so suddenly. Transport usage falls back more slowly as people are laid off or businessmen cut back on overseas trips. Likewise, the upswing is more gradual as employment and business opportunities pick up again.

Bookmakers are little affected by economic swings. Their fortunes are more closely geared to whether punters are backing the favourites. Share prices do tend to swing quite a lot but not in line with economic trends. Gambling has a hold that recession cannot shake easily.

They also do well during major sporting events such as the football World Cup, which come round at regular intervals irrespective of the global economy.

Finally, this sector has companies that are counter-cyclical, that is they disposed to do better in tough times. An example is Domino's Pizza, which sells entirely through takeways. If you cannot afford fancy restaurant prices, a takeaway pizza becomes a special treat.

So while the Industrial and Engineering index was powering away on hopes of recovery, Travel and Leisure gained a more modest 12% in the first five months of 2010, still much better than the overall market though.

Defensives

Gordon Brown, while Chancellor of the Exchequer, famously claimed to have abolished boom and bust. Events from 2007 onwards proved him wrong. We do, after all, need some recession-proof companies in our portfolio to see us through the bad times.

Defensive sectors are:

- Beverages
- Food Producers
- Heathcare
- Household Goods
- Insurance
- Pharmaceuticals
- Support Services
- Tobacco
- Water

No company is entirely recession-proof but some should, in theory, be little affected. Supermarkets spring readily to mind as an example. We do have to eat. However, we can switch to cheaper foods and drinks, thus putting pressure on the supermarkets' margins and possibly sparking damaging price wars. The diversification of products from food to clothing and electrical goods has made even these shares less recession proof.

Let us look in more detail at some typical sectors that we may wish to consider if we want to balance pour portfolio between cyclical and non-cyclical stocks.

Outsourcing companies

Outsourcing has become a buzz word over the past 20 years. Until the 1980s it was the norm for companies to run all parts of their own business, keeping control of the entire operation with various departments such as building maintenance and administration that were not part of the core business.

Gradually, however, it became fashionable to do what is popularly referred to as sticking to your knitting: doing the business you know best and leaving the peripheral stuff to the experts.

Various operations have been outsourced, most notably buildings, cleaning, catering, car fleets and IT. Smaller companies unable to afford a full time finance director have placed the running of their sales ledgers with specialists in this field.

The increasing complexity of computer technology has given the outsourcing movement a boost. Only the largest companies can keep a pool of experts on tap in-house to deal with all the issues.

Public sector outsourcing

Another important surge in outsourcing has come in the public sector, particularly since Gordon Brown took over as Chancellor in 1997. Schemes where private companies run public facilities have proliferated under various guises such as Public-Private Finance or Private Finance Initiatives.

The big advantage from government's point of view is that the private sector carries the costs in the early days, so the strain on the public purse is spread over as long as 30 years. Thus the incumbent Chancellor can keep within Budget constraints while leaving the burden to later Chancellors.

These schemes took some time to settle down. Too many private companies chased too few contracts in the early days and spent too much money bidding for work that they failed to secure.

However, the whole system has settled down well from the point of view of facilities management companies. The number of players has thinned out and the remaining ones have carved out specialist niches, for example Compass in catering services, Capita in back office functions and Connaught in street cleaning and maintaining social housing.

Compass should, in theory, be a cyclical stock – it is classified in the cyclical Travel and Leisure sector. As companies cut back on staffing levels you would assume that there are fewer meals to be served in the staff canteen.

However, catering contracts tend to be longer term so income is guaranteed not to drop off immediately. Compass thus has defensive qualities whatever its classification.

One might feel that these service providers would suffer under government cutbacks and were at risk with the change in government. Not necessarily so. All major UK political parties are heavily committed to outsourcing and it would be difficult and expensive for the government to try to wriggle out of existing contracts.

Local authorities might be planning budget cuts of up to 25% after the change of government but they are looking to private enterprises to help reduce costs while maintaining services.

Two other highly contrasting sectors spring to mind when we use the term defensive stocks. They are pharmaceuticals and tobacco.

Drugs

We do not become ill according to the economic cycle and as the population ages in the biggest markets – North America, Europe and Japan – the demand for drugs and other medical products and services will inevitably increase.

It is true that in times of recession governments will intensify efforts to reduce prices that the drug companies charge state-run health schemes, which is a reminder that all companies, however non-cyclical, are subject to some pressures during hard times.

However, competition is limited by the high costs of developing and manufacturing drugs. Stringent tests are demanded by those same governments that want to keep prices down so tests go through four phases before any drug hits the general public. It is reckoned that only one promising formula in 100 makes it onto the market.

Drug companies are also protected to some extent by patents. Recognising that the high cost of developing new products must be recouped, otherwise it will not be financially viable to carry out lengthy testing, governments have allowed new drugs to be free from competition from generic copies for several years.

However, when a patent runs out pharmas (pharmaceutical companies) find that their income from blockbuster drugs evaporates as they are forced to reduce prices to compete with copycats.

Case study: GlaxoSmithKline

Patent expiries were the curse of Glaxo coincidentally around the time of the credit crunch and the shares suffered at that time along with cyclical stocks.

The somewhat clumsily named GlaxoSmithKline owes its three capital letters to past mergers as the sector has gone through a period of consolidation, where only the strong can survive in the difficult world of creating, developing, testing, manufacturing and marketing drugs.

One of the best known brands in the business, Beecham, has disappeared from the moniker along the way, otherwise it would have been even more laborious.

Turnover at Glaxo rose steadily from £20 billion in 2004 to an estimated £29 billion in 2010, with only one small dip in 2007 and one real surge in 2009. Pre-tax profits were fairly steady during that period, hovering around £7 billion a year. Earnings per share edged upwards most years, likewise the dividend.

Dividend cover varied between 1.5 and just over two times, a little on the low side but never worryingly so considering the continually strong inward cash flow.

Glaxo's share performance over the past few years has been comparatively steady, although it has by no means been exempt from the mood in the market. Bear in mind, when looking at the Glaxo share chart, that the shares cost more than £10 each while most UK shares are priced at a much lower level. A change of 10p in a share costing 1200p is the equivalent of a 1p change in a share costing 120p.

Figure 6.4: Glaxo

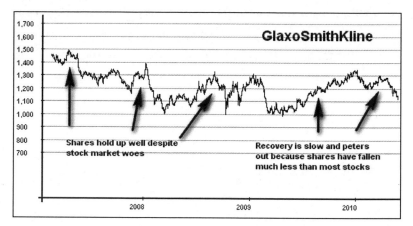

Glaxo's shares did not immediately succumb to the stock market fall that began in August 2007. Indeed, they hit a peak in January 2008, helped by their reputation as a defensive stock.

After sliding to a low of 1200p in July 2007 during a safety scare over its diabetes drug Avandia, Glaxo picked up just as other shares started to slide because profits had held up in the first half and a share buy back programme was enhancing earnings per share.

New worries over Avandia did pull the shares lower in the third quarter, a reminder that defensive stocks can have their own specific troubles, but this was offset by news that the group's cervical cancer vaccine had received marketing approval from the European Commission for all EU countries while cancer drug Tyverb performed well in phase III trials.

There was, however, no specific news to justify the spike in the share price in January 2008 nor the subsequent equally sharp fall back in the shares. No company is immune from changes in stock market sentiment.

Despite some erratic share price movements we can see that Glaxo on the whole justified its status as a defensive stock while the market in general was in freefall. The shares did hit the bottom in March 2009 as the wider market did but the recovery was much slower for Glaxo because its shares had not suffered so heavily in the downturn as cyclical stocks had.

Growth strategy

Glaxo developed a three-pronged strategy to return to growth, a strategy that in many ways changed the direction of the group without affecting its status as a defensive play.

It would continue selling pharmaceutical products into Western markets but allow this side of the business to diminish in importance: by 2010 it was down to 27% of turnover and set to fall further.

Sales of pharmaceuticals into emerging markets and the Pacific region, the second prong, were set to overtake the West, having risen to 24% of sales.

Thirdly, Glaxo was placing increasing emphasis on developing consumer goods with a health link. It already owned brands such as the Ribena and Lucozade drinks and Sensodyne toothpaste.

Glaxo also planned to cut £2.2 billion of costs from its businesses over two years to the end of 2012 although it already had a strong balance sheet with net debt of £9 billion and £7.2 billion in cash.

Tobacco

The tobacco industry, like pharmaceuticals, enjoys an ambivalent attitude from governments – although in a different form. The desire to stamp out the 'filthy habit' and reduce health costs associated with the effects of smoking are somewhat tempered by the tax revenue from the sale of cigarettes.

It is a case of: 'Oh Lord, save us from temptation, but not just yet.'

Sales in developed countries have admittedly been reduced, or at least held back, by various official assaults such as higher taxes, ever tightening controls over advertising and smoking on TV programmes, warning signs on cigarette packets and the introduction of a smoking ban in public places.

The tobacco industry is nothing if not resourceful, finding new markets to replace dwindling ones. Thus young women have stepped into the shoes of young men as the smokers of the future in the West while large markets have been carved out in the developing countries.

There has been considerable consolidation in the industry in recent years with large international groups emerging. This process has pretty much run its course with few targets left to acquire. It means that a few players are effectively carving up the global market between themselves.

As we all know, once someone has the habit, it is hard to kick it. Rising tax takes fail to deter smokers willing to pay increasing amounts to fund their need. In the Third World it is often those who can least afford it who take comfort in the weed. In times of recession tobacco offers comfort to smoker and investor alike.

Sales defy gravity

In 2009, in the teeth of the credit crunch, cigarette sales in the UK went up 1% while the French smoked 55 billion cigarettes, an increase of 3% over 2008.

It is important to compare figures for cigarettes sold rather than turnover, which can be boosted artificially by tax increases.

It is true that tobacco comes under fire with new notions for curbing the craving cropping up from time to time. The outgoing Labour government in the UK proposed plain packaging for cigarettes to discourage smoking as part of its Tobacco Control Strategy.

As the tobacco industry pointed out, such a move would encourage smuggling with the subsequent loss of revenue for the Chancellor of the Exchequer. The tobacco industry has learnt how to fight its corner over the past 50 years and the idea of plain packaging was quietly shelved.

If ever there was a non-cyclical industry, this surely is it.

Of course, those who seek ethical investments will give this sector a wide berth. It probably ranks second only to arms makers in ethical aversion. However, investors have to accept that cutting whole sectors out of their portfolios comes at the price of losing out on potential winners.

Case study: Imperial Tobacco

While Western addicts puffed away merrily, Imperial Tobacco found strong growth in emerging markets, with more cigarettes smoked in Africa and the Middle East, where Imps has been growing its market share of late. The Gauloise Blondes brand performed particularly well in Morocco.

In eastern Europe, another growth market, Imps has improved its share of most markets with sales of its Davidoff brands strong overall and Maxim gaining momentum in Russia.

It has not been all plain sailing for Imps. It borrowed heavily to buy Spanish group Altadis for £11 billion in 2008 and in 2010 its total debt stood just below that figure. However, the cash generative nature of tobacco meant that this was not too great a cause for concern and Imps was able to successfully issue £2 billion of bonds in 2009.

The Imps board made it clear that they were concentrating on controlling working capital and generating cash to strengthen the balance sheet.

Figure 6.5: Imperial Tobacco

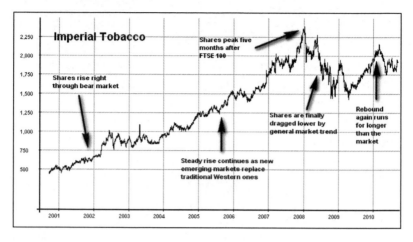

The Imperial Tobacco share chart demonstrates how defensives can buck the trend but not all the time.

The shares rose strongly to the end of 2007, turning back five months after the FTSE 100 peak, and they also tried to rally in the final quarter of 2008 against the trend. However, Imps hit the bottom in March 2009 as the main indices did before continuing its next rally further than most shares into the first quarter of 2010.

Lessons learnt

- All companies are affected to some extent by the ups and downs of the economic cycle but some are more resilient than others

- Defensive stocks tend to produce a solid but unexciting performance throughout the cycle

- Cyclicals are the companies that feel the downturn most but which also benefit most from the upturn

- Keeping abreast of the economic situation helps us to decide which shares to buy when.

Chapter 7.
Investing for Dividends

There are two components to the returns from investing in stocks: capital gains and dividends. It is easy for investors to dismiss the importance of the latter. In a bull market capital gains on stocks can be 20%, 50% or 100% – all of which can make a dividend yield of, say, 2% look rather puny by comparison. But history shows that in the longer term over half of an investor's return in the stock market comes from dividends.

Dividends are the life blood of the stock market. Just as you would refuse to put money in a savings account if the bank scrapped interest payments, the stock market would dry up if no companies paid dividends.

The general principle is that you put money into a company and reap your reward. It is true that on rare occasions a company may last for several years reinvesting all its profits and paying no dividends – provided that the investments are sound and increase profits. Ultimately, though, shareholders want something in return.

How dividends work

Each company normally pays two dividends a year, an interim after the first six months of its financial year and a final dividend after the annual general meeting. There is no set formula for how the total is divided but it is common practice for the final dividend to be roughly double the size of the interim.

A few companies pay quarterly dividends. They are generally ones with operations in the United States, where quarterly dividends are more common. Very rarely, a company may pay only a final dividend and no interim. This can happen where a small company halves the administrative cost of making two payments.

Then, alas, there are the many companies, most of them on AIM, that pay no dividend at all.

Timing

Dividends are normally declared as part of the half-yearly and annual results, which tell you the amount of the dividend per share and the date on which it will be paid. This could be several weeks later. Some companies pay up more quickly than others but they will all tend to pay on or near the same date that they paid on the previous year.

The company will also indicate on what date the shares will go ex-dividend. If you buy shares before this date you are entitled to the dividend, while if you sell you surrender the dividend to the buyer. Once the shares go ex-dividend they are traded minus the right to collect the dividend.

Companies state in their results that the dividend 'will be paid to shareholders on the register' on a specific date. That is the last date on which the shares are traded with the dividend, or 'cum dividend' as it is referred to.

Tax

The dividends will be paid net of basic rate income tax, which is deducted at source by the company. If you do not pay income tax it is too bad – you cannot get a refund.

If you are a basic rate taxpayer you must declare any dividends on your tax return but you also declare the tax credit shown on your dividend certificate, so there is nothing further to pay unless the dividends push you into a higher tax band.

Higher rate tax payers must declare dividends received and will be taxed at the higher rate minus the tax credit unless the shares are held in an ISA, in which case the dividends need not be declared and there is no further tax to pay.

Receiving dividends is straightforward. When you buy shares in a company your name goes onto a share register which is kept up-to-date by a company specialising in this service. There are several registrars operating in the UK, the most widely used being Capita, Equiniti and Share Registrars. They are paid by the company to maintain the share register and this does not involve you in any cost.

Payment

Your broker will register your shares for you and dividends will normally be posted to you as they are paid. However, your broker may hold the shares in what is called a nominee account and this will certainly happen if you buy shares as part of an ISA.

Don't worry, the shares are still in your name but dividends will be paid to you through your broker. You can arrange for the money to be:

- reinvested in the company paying the dividend (in which case it remains part of your ISA entitlement if the investment is in an ISA)
- paid into your account at the broker to pay for new investments
- or transferred to your own bank account.

Your broker will ask you which option you want when you sign up.

Assessing dividends

So what should we expect, or at least hope for, by way of dividends?

The first point is that the amount of the dividend in pence is not the criterion to go by in assessing whether to invest.

Let us take two very different companies that announce full year results in the same week in August each year. Mining group BHP Billiton announced a total dividend (interim plus final dividends) of 53p while drinks maker Diageo unveiled a total payout of 36.8p in 2010.

However, the table below illustrates that investors stood to obtain a better return from buying Diageo rather than BHP shares at this particular stage.

Company	Total dividend	Share price	£10,000 invested	Dividends received
BHP Billiton	53p	1751p	5,700 shares	£302
Diageo	36.8p	1050p	9,500 shares	£349

BHP's dividend was 44% higher than Diageo's but its share price was 67% higher, more than reflecting the higher payment per share. You got far fewer BHP shares for £10,000 invested so you stood to receive less in dividends.

We shall see why this discrepancy may have occurred as we work through this chapter. The important point is that the dividend should be considered in terms of yield on the investment and not the size of the dividend in pence.

Dividend yield

Dividend yield is expressed as a percentage. It shows how much dividend you receive for each £100 you invest. Thus the yield on BHP in our example above is 3% (53/1751) and on Diageo 3.5% (36.8/1050). The higher the yield, the better the return.

You can calculate the yield of any company as follows:

```
Dividend in pence/share price in pence X 100
```

The calculated yield may be:

- **historic** (we use the actual dividend payout for the most recent year), or

- **prospective** (we use a dividend figure based on analysts' forecasts for the current year).

It is more normal to use the prospective (also called *future*) yield. We are not interested in what the company has already paid out except as a guide to the future. What we are interested in is what we stand to gain from our investment over the next 12 months and beyond.

Note, there is little need to calculate the yield for yourself: daily newspapers and websites carrying share prices include yields in their stock market tables.

The question is: what constitutes an acceptable yield?

As a ball park figure, and it is a pretty big park, we would expect something in the region of 3 to 3.5%. We normally expect dividend yields to be lower than interest on savings accounts or on bonds because share prices and dividends tend to rise over time, so we have a capital gain on top of our growing dividend.

Since shares tend to perform better over time, and thus offer greater rewards than other forms of investment, the immediate returns reflect the relationship between risk and reward: the more you stand to gain in the future, the more you have to pay to join the club now.

When, as can happen, yields on ordinary shares rise above yields on bonds, it is a signal to consider buying shares. It means that investors have rushed into bonds as a perceived safer haven: companies pay bondholders their fixed rate of interest before they set the dividend for shareholders. If there is not enough cash to go round, the dividend can be reduced.

You have to take a judgement on whether the fears are overdone. If the market has overreacted, shares will soon start to rise to balance out the possible risks and potential rewards.

Why dividend yields fluctuate

Dividend yields do fluctuate. The yield for any company will rise if the company's shares fall or its dividend is increased: conversely the yield falls when the shares price rises or the dividend is reduced. Since share prices usually fluctuate on a daily basis, the yield will vary from day to day. The yield can also change dramatically if the dividend is raised or reduced.

Dividend yields for the market generally tend to **rise** when:

- interest rates are rising. Investments such as savings accounts and bonds become more attractive while borrowing money to finance share buying becomes less attractive

- the economic outlook is uncertain. Investors fear that profits will fall

- analysts are expected to reduce profit forecasts.

Dividend yields tend to **fall** when:

- interest rates are falling, making alternative investments less attractive

- the economic outlook is improving, raising hopes for company profits and dividends

- investors sense that analysts will raise their forecasts.

As a general principle, we look for shares with the highest prospective yields.

Guidelines on yields

It would be wonderful to point to certain types of share and say with certainty that these are the ones offering the best prospects for investors looking for dividends, but watertight rules are not the nature of the stock market. In any case, investors will tend to buy shares in the best run companies, pushing down their yields and spurning the biggest risks, so a high yield often indicates poorer prospects.

There are, though, some general rules and the two most important are these:

1. The market *usually* gets it right

2. The market is *not always* right.

Share prices do go up and down to reflect changing prospects. Some shares and some sectors are highly rated for good reason while investors can usually sniff out a dud. So much information has to be announced to the market that it is hard to disguise good or bad news.

Nonetheless, opportunities do arise where good companies escape the notice of larger investors or overrated companies stay in favour despite warning signs.

Here are some more general rules:

- Larger companies are less likely to scrap their dividends than smaller ones. The majority of shares quoted on AIM do not pay a dividend. On the other hand, companies do not last for long in the FTSE 100 if they go for more than a couple of years without rewarding their shareholders. It is true that Royal Bank of Scotland and Lloyds both suspended their dividends in the aftermath of the banking crisis while BP suspended payments after its disastrous Gulf of Mexico oil spill. However, with larger companies, there is an expectation that they will soon recommence dividends.

- Defensive companies offer better prospects of steady dividend payments than cyclical ones. All companies try to raise their dividends a little each year, or at least maintain them at a constant level, and this is much easier if revenue and profits do not bounce up and down.

- Companies with a steady record of making increased profits over at least five years are more likely to continue to make payments.

- Companies that have recently returned to profit after several years of making losses are unlikely to pay a dividend until the directors are satisfied that the bad times are over.

Dividends are never 100% safe. They are, however, rarely suspended and are not often reduced. This is because directors prefer not to disappoint investors, partly for fear of losing their jobs. Thus a maiden dividend will not be introduced at a company unless the board is reasonably satisfied that it can be continued.

The company will have built up reserves to smooth out the dividend payments so generally speaking dividends are scrapped only when it is clear that losses will persist. Otherwise the dividend can be paid wholly or in part out of reserves.

The best prospects are those companies that:

- pay a dividend that is covered at least twice by earnings per share (eps). The earnings figure will be given in the results and should be sufficient to pay the dividend and leave a similar amount to be added to reserves or fund expansion of the business

- have a strong inward cash flow sufficient to fund the dividend. You can see how much the dividend is costing in total and how much cash has come in by checking the balance sheet issued with annual results

- are solid and boring. High fliers have a tendency to crash to earth as rapidly as they soared.

The key figure we are looking for when investing for dividends, though, is the yield, and the higher the better. A high yield means a larger return on our investment.

As always, a little caution and a great deal of common sense is required. We should ask ourselves why other investors have not cottoned onto this juicy return. Is there some worry in the market that we have overlooked?

It is possible that other investors fear that profits in the current and future years will fall short of past performance. If there are concerns about current trading conditions then analysts may reduce their dividend forecasts, which will downgrade prospective yields.

Alongside this we should consider what is *not* particularly important to dividend investors. We do not really care how the share price has moved in the past or how it is likely to move in the future. These are considerations for short term traders looking to make profits from buying and selling rather than sitting back and enjoying income.

It is very gratifying if shares we buy do rise in value but, unless we want to sell, this is a gain purely on paper.

A similar situation arises when we buy a house: it is consoling to think that we could sell it at a profit but what use is that if we do not want to move? Even if we do want to move, our next purchase will cost us correspondingly more so the gain is wiped out.

If you invest for income, you will not want to sell even at a profit unless you see a better prospect and you do not have the ready cash to snap it up.

It will be extremely temping to look at the share price chart of a company with a high yield and be distracted by the fact that the shares have already risen strongly. You then decide not to invest because the shares might run out of steam.

What does it matter? You are investing for dividends, not capital gains. Your concern is whether you are buying a high yielding share with good prospects that the dividend will be maintained. Get that right and the share price will look after itself.

Where to look for dividends

We have noted that prospects for individual companies and entire sectors will change from time to time, but to illustrate what we are looking for let us take some examples as they applied in the summer of 2010. The points raised will still have relevance in subsequent years.

Electricity

The electricity sector had a couple of useful possibilities in the shape of energy supplier National Grid and the second largest electricity generator Scottish & Southern Energy. Private investors had already recognised the attractions of utilities by switching heavily into the sector in the early part of 2010.

National Grid had also seen its shares plunge, but for a rather different reason. It had recently made a successful but substantial rights issue to raise cash to invest in its UK transmission business. (We shall look at this in more detail in a later chapter.)

While the rights issue was unpopular, especially as National Grid had previously indicated that it would have enough cash for investment without one, it was taken up by 95% of shareholders after receiving enthusiastic endorsements from analysts and the press.

National Grid had committed itself to increasing its dividend by 8% a year for the following two years, which put the shares on a forward P/E of 10.7 and a prospective yield of 6.9%, nearly double the stock market average of 3.65% at that time.

Apart from generating electricity, Scottish & Southern has a large mechanical and electrical contracting business and was in the process of buying North Sea gas and infrastructure assets, giving it a wider base.

There were also plans to invest £6.7 billion over the following five years, mainly in renewable energy, supply networks and gas storage.

The yield was at that stage already attractive at 6.5% but the icing on the cake was a promise to raise the payout by at least two percentage points above the rate of inflation for three years. After that the dividend would continue to grow faster than inflation.

Telecoms

Telecoms giant Vodafone similarly had indicated its intention to grow the dividend, in its case by 7% a year for three years, which was the size of the increase in 2009. The yield stood at 6.4% with the prospect of much more to come.

There were admittedly one or two issues with Vodafone. While the group's operations in Northern Europe were improving, the economic problems for countries around the Mediterranean threatened to cut cash flow from this part of the Eurozone.

Vodafone had a 45% stake in Verizon Wireless in the US which had not paid a dividend for five years. Verizon did have cash flowing in but chose to use the proceeds to reduce debt, a process likely to be completed by the end of 2010.

Thus there were genuine prospects that Vodafone could start to cash in on this investment soon. Verizon indicated in mid-2010 that it expected to start dividend payments in 2012.

Insurance

In the insurance sector, Aviva offered a yield of 7%, Standard Life 6.5% and RSA 6.6%. These are all substantial companies and those yields are based on 2009 figures, allowing scope for improvement in 2010 and beyond.

RSA for one was expected to raise its dividend by 7% in 2010. Its balance sheet was strong and it was expected to show a steady if unspectacular level of profitability, indicators that the dividend would be at least maintained.

Nearly 90% of RSA's investment portfolio was in high quality fixed income and cash assets and its exposure to sovereign debt in Southern Europe was minimal.

Net written premiums were up 5% in the first three months of 2010, including a 5% increase in emerging markets. In the UK, where growth was running at an impressive 7%, RSA had struck a deal with supermarket group Tesco to offer pet insurance through Tesco Bank.

RSA had managed to increase prices of insurance premiums over several quarters by this stage while reducing costs.

The insurance sector admittedly has a tendency to go through cycles of feast and famine. In the good years more players scramble for lucrative business until the market becomes saturated and premiums are driven down to unrealistic levels. The sector then becomes unprofitable, the weak players are driven out and premiums rise again.

Nonetheless, this cycle has not been as severe as it was in the 1990s and the bigger companies are now international entities with a good spread of business, so a downturn in one area can be offset by better trading conditions elsewhere.

Also, the new found wealth of Asian countries such as China and India has opened up new markets with enormous potential for growth as they are virtually untapped.

Other dividend payers

Multinational pharmaceutical companies such as GlaxoSmithKline and AstraZeneca have traditionally been strong dividend payers. GSK shares had already risen to anticipate a sharp rise in its dividend so its yield based on the past year was only 2%. Astra was on a yield of 3.1% at this stage but within the same sector Shire stood out with a yield of 8.3%.

Companies producing consumer goods were particularly popular with investors by mid-2010 and Unilever, the Anglo-Dutch maker of washing up liquids and basic foods, was yielding nearly 4%.

It was seen as a company that could deliver growth against a weak economic background with big selling brands such as Dove, Persil, Colman's mustard and Wall's ice cream.

Dividend cuts

We have noted that there are inevitably phases where dividends are reduced, not only for individual companies but, more rarely, across the board.

After the global recession in 2007-9, dividends were heavily slashed. There was a lagging effect. It took time for the impact of the banking crash and the credit crunch to feed through into lower dividends.

Companies are reluctant to reduce payouts, as these are so important to investors, especially those who rely on dividends as their main income. Cutting the dividend carries a certain degree of opprobrium for directors, carrying as it does an unspoken implication that they have not done their job properly.

So the brunt of dividend reductions did not feed through until 2009 and was still being felt in the first quarter of 2010, when payouts totalling £13.6 billion were 2.5% lower than in the first quarter of 2009.

The stock market is pretty accurate at foreseeing these changes, though. Having fallen heavily in late 2007, throughout 2008 and into the first two months of 2009, the recovery in shares began in early March 2009 and continued right through to the end of the year even as dividends were being trimmed back.

The first quarter is important because it includes virtually all those companies using the calendar year as their year end. Some 186 companies paid dividends in the first three months of 2010, up from 161 in the same period of 2009 despite the lower total overall.

Dividends restored

While 56 companies cut or cancelled their payouts, 30 held them unchanged and 102 increased or reinstated their dividends. This reflects an important point. When a company decides it cannot afford to maintain the previous year's level of payment it will tend to bite the bullet and cut heavily so the bad news is over in one go. When dividends are restored the company will be naturally cautious to avoid further ignominy if recovery is slow.

It was instructive that during early 2010 the range of companies restoring the dividend was quite wide, indicating that recovery was across the board. Among those returning to the dividend lists were cruise operator Carnival, Barclays bank and miner Rio Tinto. At the same time supermarket chain Morrison and retailer Next raised their payouts by more than 20%.

High payers

At times of widespread cuts in dividends it is particularly useful to look for stocks with a dividend yield that is greater than average for their respective sectors but where the dividend is well covered by earnings, preferably at least two times. This removes, or at least greatly reduces, the possibility of the dividend being cut if earnings fall short of expectations.

Look also for dividend growth – that is, has the dividend increased year by year? This is an indication that the company has a strong balance sheet and relatively resilient cash flow. It can be a sign that the company has been able to trade through difficult times as well as the boom years.

Sometimes it is possible to foresee whether a dividend will be reintroduced. For instance, it was clear that Royal Bank of Scotland and Lloyds Bank would not be bringing back dividends until they had severed their reliance on government support.

Dividends in dollars

Investors should bear in mind that globalisation means many of the top UK companies declare dividends in dollars, which means they can be artificially inflated or deflated when translated into sterling according to fluctuations in the pound/dollar exchange rate.

This affects not just the large foreign-based companies but also the likes of BP, Shell, HSBC and AstraZeneca. Setting the dividend in dollars can make sense if your income is international. For oil companies, the whole industry operates in dollars from the moment the stuff comes out of the ground.

In contrast, retailers such as Sainsbury, Home Retail, Halfords, N Brown and many in other sectors, including bookmaker William Hill, drinks maker Britvic, support services specialist WS Atkins and insurer Legal & General, rely mainly on domestic business.

Lessons learnt

- When investing for income the key figure we look at is the yield

- The higher the yield the greater the return on our investment – provided that the dividend is maintained or increased

- A high yield may indicate that investors fear that the dividend will be reduced.

Chapter 8.
Investing for Capital Growth

The alternative to investing for dividends is to seek to make capital gains by buying shares cheaply and selling at a profit.

This strategy tends to appeal to:

- younger people hoping to build a nest egg rather than retired folk looking for income to boost their pensions

- active investors who seek to cash in on share price gains and find new targets

- those willing to admit when they made a mistake and are prepared to cut their losses

- investors with sufficient capital to trade through lean times

- keen followers of economic news who monitor the impact of factors such as changing interest rates and unemployment figures

- those who have already built a portfolio for income and now feel free to build a separate portfolio with different objectives

- anyone with an eye for a bargain.

Investors for capital growth will be more interested in price/earnings ratios than yields, although yields can be a useful additional guide to spotting undervalued companies. The lower the P/E, the cheaper the company – although investors should always bear in mind that a company may be cheap for a good reason.

The average P/E for fully listed shares in London tends to average about 13 times earnings. The figure will be lower in tough economic times as investors fear a reduction in earnings; it will be higher in boom times as investors factor increased earnings into their calculations.

You should target shares in companies that:

- are making sound profits but have a lower than average P/E ratio

- are not making a profit but are about to move into the black

- are too small to attract the interest of investment funds but have scope for long term growth

- have seen their shares rise recently and look to have further to go.

Investors seeking capital gains will be much more interested in whether shares are cyclical or defensive. While investors seeking income can ride out the ups and downs of the stock market as long as their holdings continue to pay a dividend, capital gains investors try to anticipate the cycle.

For this reason you will be more interested in the share price chart than is the case for income investors. If the shares have fallen recently, are they turning the corner? If they have risen, are they running out of steam or do they have further to go?

Note the danger of incurring capital gains tax if, as you would hope to do, you make more than £10,100 profit from buying and selling shares in any one tax year. You can ameliorate the impact by using your annual ISA allowance of £10,200 but once you have sold shares in your ISA you cannot replace them with new investments.

Growth companies

It is reasonable to argue that every portfolio should have at least one growth company in its ranks – indeed one could construct an entire portfolio of growth companies.

After all, the argument goes, we are surely looking for companies with a bit of go about them. We hardly want stagnant, unambitious companies in our portfolio. We want companies that are gaining market share, outdoing their rivals and building profits.

As always on the stock market, life is never so clear cut. Growth companies are likely to have their sparkling prospects reflected in the share price. Unless you can catch a growth company in its early stages the scope for breathtaking gains is seriously reduced.

Nonetheless, many investors who follow share price charts closely will be happy with this situation. They would argue that it is all right to miss the first stages of a soaring share price as long as you are in for the best part of the ride.

This is a perfectly reasonable argument. Rises (and falls) in share prices tend to continue for longer than you expect. If you missed the first half of a share price surge, why miss the second half as well?

The downside is that one day all growth companies hit the buffers. Stock market darlings such as plant hire group Speedy Hire and builders' merchant Wolseley came a cropper. We shall look at Wolseley in more detail later.

In more extreme cases the company can be so overextended that it runs out of cash. A prime example was a Lancashire cake maker called Inter Link. Its shares soared as it gobbled up smaller rivals but, completely out of the blue, it ran into difficulties. Within weeks the company folded, leaving investors with nothing.

Growth companies are, therefore, mainly for more active traders while long term traders prefer solid, less spectacular performance. You have to be prepared to get out as well as getting in.

Value investing

One often hears of value investing as if it is some sort of mysterious formula for turning base metal into gold. It simply means buying assets that are undervalued and holding on to them until the market realises their true value and we can sell at a profit before going off to look for the next bargain.

But isn't that what we are all trying to do, you may ask. Yes of course it is. Don't let glib phrases bamboozle you.

Value is often misused as a euphemism for cheap. We hear of 'value retailers' such as Primark or Asda in contrast to Marks & Spencer or Waitrose, as if M&S and Waitrose did not provide value. A Rolls-Royce is value if you can afford one. Otherwise we settle for a Ford or a Fiat, not because they are better value but because they are cheaper.

In retailing it is easy to see what is cheap because we can visit several shops selling the same items and see which T shirt or cheesecake has the lowest price tag. But price is not the same as value: the cheapest T shirt may fall apart at the seams after a couple of outings while the cheesecake may taste unpleasant.

We must adapt the same critical eye to so-called 'value investments'. Shares are not cheap, or good value, just because they are low in price. In any case, as with goods in the shops, they may be cheap simply because they are of lower value.

Case Study: Dogs of the Dow

As an example of a strategy designed to produce capital gains, we will look at the O'Higgins formula, also fondly known as the Dogs of the Dow.

As the epithet implies, Michael O'Higgins applied his theory to US stocks but the principle can be adapted to any established stock market and it translates easily to the London Stock Exchange.

He selected the ten companies in the Dow Jones Industrial Average with the highest prospective yields and suggested investing equal amounts in the five with the lowest price in dollars. Thus he found the elusive goal of trying to select high yield, low risk stocks – the stock market's equivalent of turning base metal into gold.

His argument was that these are the least well regarded stocks (in the index, the 'dogs' that lack appeal. because their high yields indicate that their share prices are unusually low relative to the level of their dividend payouts). These are thus the cheapest stocks available, offering the best chance of recovery if in fact projected dividends turn into reality. O'Higgins argued that the market overdoes the gloom in these situations.

The stocks that emerge from a selection system such as this are those that the market has written off, forgotten about, or believes are so financially insecure that they may be planning to cut their dividends. The danger is that they do in fact cut their dividends, but that is a risk you have to take. At least with five stocks there is a chance that four will come good even if one lets you down.

To give the system time to work, he advocated leaving the investments in place for 12 months, at which stage the exercise can be repeated. You can then reconstruct the portfolio by cashing in those shares that came good and replacing them with new 'dogs'.

The hard bit is leaving the shares undisturbed for 12 months. This runs counter to all the arguments that you should keep an eye on your portfolio and take action as circumstances change. It is certainly an ideal method for those who do simply want to close their eyes and hope for the best.

The system is suitable for investors seeking capital gains as well as income from dividends. Assuming that the dividends materialise as promised, the share price will presumably rise accordingly.

Note that there is a danger that you will run up a capital gains tax liability when you sell off the stocks that have recovered.

Refining O'Higgins

If you find the O'Higgins method of whittling ten dogs down to five a little arbitrary, alternatives are to take the five with the highest yields or those among the ten dogs with the lowest price/earnings ratios, another indication that the shares are undervalued.

The reasons why O'Higgins chose the Dow rather than the market in general are:

- These are comparatively large companies and are unlikely to go bust

- The index contains long standing companies with a track record

- They are the subject of greater attention from analysts than smaller, lesser known, companies and therefore we get a wider range of projections

- They are not covered only by the house broker so research is unbiased.

Another advantage is that share prices of companies in the main index in any country are more readily available in the press so it is easy to keep tabs on them.

The same arguments apply to the FTSE 100 index so this method of stock picking applies equally well in the UK. And while the Dow has only 30 component companies concentrated in the Industrial sector, the FTSE has more than three times as many companies spread across a wider range of businesses.

You can easily find which shares are in the FTSE 100. They are listed on the London Stock Exchange website and on financial websites such as Hemscott, Digital Look, ADVFN, Yahoo and Motley Fool.

Alternatively, newspapers carrying lists of stock market prices usually distinguish the blue chips by printing them in bold type.

While you have to plough through a long list, the advantage of looking in the papers is that the tables carry prospective yields so you can easily pick out the ones with the highest figures.

Single stocks

O'Higgins argued that his system works equally well for selecting a single stock. In this case you take the 'dog' with the second lowest share price. Again this is a rather arbitrary decision but that is what O'Higgins decided.

You can try a more scientific selection of a single stock if you wish, but the creator of the system claimed that his selections outperformed the market on average by more than five percentage points each year taking into account dividends paid and changes in share prices.

Testing the method

Various publications and websites in the UK, including the *Financial Times,* the *Investors' Chronicle* and Hemscott, have put this method to the test with encouraging results. It seems to work best when markets are recovering as in 2003, when the selections had double digit yields, but it works less well in slowly rising markets and fares worst in falling markets.

The *Investors' Chronicle* tested the method for five years from 2005 to 2009, with spectacular results for the final year when the market recovered strongly from the credit crunch crash.

The five stocks the system selected at the end of 2008 (GKN, Logica, ITS, BT and Ladbrokes) rose on average by 41.9%. That compares with a gain in the market of 22.1%. On top of this, the average yield on the group was 11.1%, giving a total return over the course of the year of over 50%.

Likewise O'Higgins scored share price gains of 117% in the bull market of 2005 against an overall market gain of 24%, and 42% against an overall gain of 16% in 2007.

Not so good was 2006, with a gain of 5% compared with the market's 11%, and 2008 with a fall of 50% as the market tumbled by 34%.

However, the magazine had not counted in the dividends, which in all years were above average, so the returns on this tactic were more favourable than the bare figures show.

Lessons learnt

- The price/earnings ratio is the key factor when investing for capital gains

- A low P/E indicates that the shares are cheap

- Check whether there is a good reason why the shares are so cheap before plunging in

- Look at the share chart to see whether the trend is up or down. Remember that share price trends tend to run on longer than you expect and are often followed by a correction.

Chapter 9.
When to Invest

The curse of the private investor is that he or she tends to buy when prices are high and sell when they are lower, the very antithesis of what should happen. We should be looking to buy when share prices have fallen.

But, human nature being what it is, we all want to jump on the bandwagon after a strong rise in share prices and to back off in trepidation as they fall.

It is true that we do not want to risk our money in a bear market that has further to run, but our attitude should be that lower share prices offer a better opportunity to invest. We get more shares for our money.

Bull or bear market

One way of assessing whether we are in a bull or a bear market is a surprisingly simple one: which holds greater sway, the good news or the bad news?

There are times when each piece of bad news causes a one day fall in the stock market whereas each piece of good news leads to the recovery of those losses and more besides. The market can in fact shrug off quite dire trade, budget deficit, unemployment or inflation figures and resume its rise a day later.

When this happens we are still in a bull market.

Conversely, when a piece of good news sends shares temporarily higher and the response in the market is to take profits while the chance is there, we are in a bear market. In these circumstances each piece of bad news sends shares lower until the next silver lining produces a temporary reprieve.

Volatile markets

One tends to think of volatile markets as being ideal for short term investors and too dangerous for long term share buying, but we shall see that this is not the case.

There is an old adage that markets hate uncertainties. Rubbish! What the markets hate is being in the doldrums. The more movement there is in share prices, the more scope there is to make decent profits.

Short termism in particular thrives on short, sharp changes in the markets. If you are looking for a quick profit on top of your dealing costs then clearly you need a fair swing in share prices during the course of a trading day to make any money.

However, this is dangerous because if you make the wrong call you are badly out of pocket. Short term traders gain at someone else's short term loss. Since dealing costs come into the equation, this is not a zero sum game where total gains equal total losses. Overall, more is lost than gained and only the stock brokers win.

On the other hand, volatile conditions create ideal buying opportunities. Yes, it can be scary, but if you are buying for the long term you should not be too worried about temporary setbacks. Falls in share prices are significant to you only if the market is in long term freefall. Even then, if your time frame is long enough, you can sit tight until the next bull market.

Buying opportunities

We are back to the old conundrum: buyers should buy in falling rather than rising markets. Unfortunately we all prefer to buy in rising markets, where each gain on the shares we already own spurs us on to buy more goodies and each fall fills us with horror at the ghastly mistake we fear we have made.

Case study: FTSE 100, June 2007 to June 2010

Let us look at events between June 2007 and June 2010 as an illustration. I have chosen this period because it incorporated the end of a bull market, a long bear phase, a period of months in which the market went violently sideways, an unexpectedly strong rally and a period of daily volatility.

For more than a year from June 2007 the markets reacted belatedly to the crisis in the financial sector. Usually stock markets are ahead of the game, factoring in good or bad news quickly in response to economic news and often anticipating events.

However, the scale of the sub-prime mortgage scandal caught markets on the hop. Perhaps people had difficultly in believing the sheer scale of the crisis or maybe it was the fact that the banks themselves had little idea of the risks they were taking.

So although the crisis had been developing since the beginning of 2007, it was not until August that year that the FTSE 100 index peaked at 6754 points.

Figure 9.1: FTSE 100

Chasing the market higher after the best gains have been made is what small investors unfortunately do well. Many who were scared off after three years of falling share prices at the start of the millennium were lured back in as the index neared 6000 points and talk was of the market doubling from its low of 3200 points in March 2003. Perhaps we would even see the all-time peak of just under 7000 points broken.

Alas, the market finally faced reality and by October 2008 the FTSE was down to around 4000 points and seemingly in freefall. It was reasonable for investors to stay out of the market, even though shares had become cheaper. It was not at all clear where the market would settle and it was wise to exercise caution.

Yet now was the time for selective buying – selective in terms of when, not what, to buy. For six months shares bounced around between a floor of 3800 points and a ceiling of 4400 points.

Worries were:

- The banking crisis was still running its course and it was still unclear how serious the situation was

- Memories of the dot.com boom and bust, which led to a three-year bear market, were sufficiently fresh in investors' memories

- Stock markets had been falling all over the world, indicating dangers of a global meltdown, so it was impossible to find any companies even partly immune from the crisis.

It was therefore entirely forgivable, prudent even, to baulk when the market first hit the floor. However, after several shifts between the two limits it gradually became clear that it was worth buying shares below 4000 points and best to hold off above 4000.

There was, admittedly, a danger in this strategy. Eventually the market was likely to break out of the sideways trend with a whoosh and no-one could be sure whether it would be an up or down whoosh.

Furthermore, any downward movement was likely to be sharp. If the FTSE 100 index dropped below its support level then panic would inevitably have set in and the index might well have plunged to its previous low of 3200 points.

In contrast, any upward movement seemed doomed to be anaemic given the scale of the financial crisis.

Why it looked right to buy

Yet it always looked more likely that the market would recover in due course because:

- stock markets around the world had factored a lot of bad news into share prices
- markets around the world had stabilised
- governments around the world had taken daring, decisive action to contain the crisis.

Yes, there were risks but then there is always risk, whatever you do with your money.

In the event, fortune favoured the brave and the strength of the upward surge in share prices took most commentators by surprise.

Correction overdue

By the end of the year, however, with the FTSE up to 5600 points, it was time to be more circumspect. Again, this was a time when those who had been left behind were belatedly piling in for fear they were missing their chance to join the fun. Alas, they had already missed their chance.

Shares had, on average, risen by 40% from the bottom and the speed of the rise was a warning to hold back, not pile in. Whenever the stock market rises strongly over a period of several months there is almost always a correction – that is, a moderate fall in share prices, time to give investors chance to catch their breath.

It is at this point that traders who look to the medium term take their profits, hoping to buy back in at a lower level. The surprise on this occasion was that the correction took so long to happen. Cautious investors could have been forgiven for cashing in sooner, given that the economic situation still gave cause for concern.

Smaller companies turn first

There was a subtle warning sign. Although all the main indices had hit the bottom on 3rd March 2009, it is unusual for the whole market to turn a corner at the same time. Surprisingly, it is the smaller end of the main market and AIM that tend to change tack first rather than the largest companies leading the way.

The Small Cap index and the AIM index came off the top in October 2009, although the FTSE 100 continued to gain ground until the end of the calendar year.

The first half of 2010 brought a new phase for investors with strong swings, up and down, on many trading days. Just as the swings between 3800 and 4400 points had presented investors with buying opportunities over a period of months, there were buying opportunities on a weekly basis.

Investors were spooked by the sovereign debt crisis in Europe as it become clear that countries such as Greece, Italy, Portugal and Spain were running up unsustainable levels of government debt in contravention of Eurozone rules. Because these countries were members of the single currency they could not solve their economic woes by currency devaluation.

Bitter medicine was forced initially on Greece despite rioting in the street. Spain took its own medicine rather more voluntarily but the prospect of a collapse in the euro, with countries possibly being forced out, caused nervous spasms along the way. Consequently it was not unusual to see swings of more than 1%, and sometimes as much as 2%, in one day.

Each downswing was a signal to consider buying. Each upswing was a warning to stand back.

Pound cost averaging

Since swings in share prices can be unpredictable we may take a deliberate decision to spread share purchases over a period of time. You decide to invest equal pound amounts in a stock at regular intervals (e.g. £200 every month) irrespective of whether the shares go up or down in the meantime.

Some expert and successful investors argue that, since you are unlikely to choose exactly the right moment to invest, given the volatile nature of the stock market, spreading purchases is a sensible approach. If you invest the same amount each time then you will buy more shares when they are cheap and fewer when they are expensive.

The main drawback is that by making several purchases you multiply the dealing costs. At a flat rate cost of £10 a trade, which is the minimum you are likely to find, five purchases cost you £40 more than one purchase. That extra £40 has to be recouped in dividends or a rising share price.

Portfolio

It is perfectly legitimate to decide, for budgetary reasons, to invest a fixed amount each month in your portfolio as a whole. You may not have a lump sum to invest but perhaps you have regular income and feel that you can commit, say, £200 a month to share purchases after taking into consideration your other outgoings. It makes perfect sense to build your holdings over time.

In such circumstances your best tactic is to invest the full amount available in just one stock rather than try to spread the butter too thinly because:

- you will concentrate on finding the best current prospect among the companies you wish to invest in

- you keep dealing costs to a minimum.

Savings plans

If your money is very tight you should consider setting up a savings plan with an investment trust so that you can dribble in money at a regular monthly rate and spread your risk across a wide range of shares.

This does rather take away the fun of running your own portfolio as you hand the investment decisions to a manager but it does get you into the market. This could also form a solid, regular investment to run alongside your main share portfolio, providing a cushion in turbulent trading conditions.

Lessons learnt

- Aim to buy at the bottom of the market and sell at the top – most small investors contrive to do the opposite!

- Smaller shares tend to turn the corner first when a bull or bear market comes to an end

- Look for the point when all the bad news seems to have been factored into a bear market or all the good news into a bull market – that is when markets are likely to turn

- Major stock markets around the world tend to move in the same direction so be cautious if the UK market is bucking the trend.

Chapter 10.
New Issues

The timing of new issues raises a note of caution for investors. While takeover bids tend to congregate near the bottom of the market, where companies can be picked up relatively cheaply, new issues are almost invariably pitched into a rising market and suggest confidence in the immediate future.

Be warned, though: they can signal that share prices are approaching a peak.

The reason is that company owners will wish to maximise the amount raised, either for the company itself or for the owners if they are reducing their stakes. It is much easier to persuade private and institutional investors to cough up if there is reasonable hope that an established bull market will continue.

Investors who have taken profits from selling shares at high prices will be looking for somewhere to park their cash. New issues offer just such an option.

You will therefore tend to find that after a bear market there is a pile of new issues waiting for an auspicious time to flood out onto the market.

The lessons of 2010

This was particularly true in 2010. The bear market of 2007-9 caused by the credit crunch and the near-collapse of the global economy was followed by a period of volatile conditions on the London and other stock markets. Privately-owned companies and their advisers were reluctant to take the plunge for fear that the issue would bomb.

We might have expected a rush of new issues in the first couple of months of the year after the surprisingly resilient bull phase starting in March 2009 and running right round to January 2010. Indeed, one or two brave souls such as fashion retailer New Look and hotel and airline booking company Travelport did put their heads above the parapet, only to withdraw ignominiously a couple of weeks later after investors raised concerns about aspects of the companies.

New Look ran into immediate scepticism over its high levels of debt (see case study); Travelport had a generous executive incentive scheme, flying in the face of criticism over bonus schemes after massive payouts to those who precipitated the banking debacle.

That two such companies should emerge first from the pile was a surprise. One would have expected an adviser somewhere to trot out a really top drawer company to get the show on the road. The tentative and, in the event, temporary offers that we did get indicated considerable uncertainty behind the scenes.

However, the longer the delay the greater the logjam waiting to pile onto the market and the wider the range of sectors that would eventually be on offer. By the time the general election had come and gone we had these companies and more waiting in the wings:

- Suek – Russia's biggest coal company with a potential cap of £8 billion

- Flybe – a regional airline worth about £400 million

- Ocado – the home delivery firm for supermarket chain Waitrose valued at more than £1 billion

- Merlin Entertainments – owner of Alton Towers and Tussauds, hoping to revive a £2 billion float abandoned earlier in the year as markets turned down

- Betfair – an online betting exchange considering a £1.5 billion float.

This list was more what we would expect after a long period without floats: a fair cross section of substantial companies.

Taken on merit

Each float has to be considered on its merits. While we would expect the most promising companies to come to market in the first surge, because advisers will want one or two early successes to buoy the market, there is no guarantee that the frontrunners will be better than the chasing pack.

To be sure, executives who are on the ball will want to float early in the cycle before most of the cash is mopped up. They and their advisers will have worked out details such as how many shares will be issued, the price range, and what the cash will be used for so that a float can be launched at a few days' notice.

Conversely, the late comers should be looked at with a more critical eye. Are they just trying to jump on the bandwagon while the going is good? When you see companies of lesser quality joining the tail end of a listings queue, we could be coming to the end of the bull phase.

Pricing

The theory in an initial public offering (IPO) is that shares should be priced just below their true market value. The aim is to raise the full amount of money that the company needs for expansion or to give its private owners an exit without issuing more shares than is necessary. The current owners will probably be retaining a stake, so they will not want to dilute their own holding more than is necessary.

Advisers to the float will prefer to settle the price just slightly on the low side. This allows for some margin of error in case investors are reluctant to stump up, perhaps because the stock market turns down before they can get the issue away or because there is discouraging news within the sector the company operates in.

No adviser wants the ignominy of seeing the shares drop below the issue price immediately after the IPO. Once a company's shares start to fall back from the float price they tend to drift for weeks or months.

For this reason new issues used to be considered a great investment as share buyers were virtually guaranteed an instant capital gain. Buying shares in IPOs and selling quickly at a profit is known as *stagging* and it was a particularly popular pastime in the days of privatisations, when very large issues had to be attractively priced because of the sheer amount of money they were mopping up.

Pricing the shares to maximise the cash raised without scaring off potential investors is a highly skilled art and advisers, being human, do not always get it right.

Besides, issuing shares to the general public is time consuming and expensive, involving the issuing of a bulky prospectus, collecting in and counting the applications, cashing the cheques, refunding those who do not get their full allocation when the issue is oversubscribed and, above all, paying underwriters to take the rump of the shares if the issue is undersubscribed.

Book building

It has become increasingly common, therefore, for IPOs to be made through a *book building* exercise that unfortunately tends to freeze out small private investors. Advisers approach institutional investors and ask them how many shares they would be prepared to buy and at what price. Fewer prospectuses have to be printed and sent out; the market price for the shares can be calculated easily and underwriting fees are avoided.

If an IPO is made in this fashion you can only shrug your shoulders and move on. It is perfectly legal and within stock exchange rules. It is just possible that your stock broker will be able to bundle up applications from you and other clients and endeavour to secure an allocation but don't count on it. This is one area of stock market investing where the playing field is not level.

When you are allowed to invest, you will almost certainly be obliged to commit yourself before you know how much the shares are going to cost you. This is because the retail offer closes before the bookbuilding is complete.

This is not as risky as it sounds. Firstly, you will have a fair idea of the price range from reading newspaper reports of the float. Secondly, you will be paying the same price as the institutions.

In any case, the more efficient the pricing is, the less scope there is for stagging. It is not such a big deal to be frozen out.

Admittedly, the share price is likely to rise a little after the float as those investors who missed out try to buy their way in.

However, it is generally better to let the shares settle after the first flush of enthusiasm. It is true that they may continue to until and you have missed your chance to get in. More likely, though, they will settle back giving investors an opportunity to buy in. It is possible that they will fall away badly.

Case study: Debenhams

High street store chain Debenhams returned to the stock market in the middle of 2006 after two-and-a-half years in private ownership. At this stage the problems of sub-prime mortgages that ultimately engulfed the finance sector had not emerged. The stock market still had further to rise and the flotation of Debenhams initially looked reasonably auspicious.

Debenhams was taken private in December 2003 by private equity investors who paid £1.5 billion. They stripped out costs but they also stripped out cash, a tactic often used by private equity investors looking for juicy returns: the store chain had £100 million of debt when it was taken private and it returned owing £1.2 billion.

It thus now depended on strong profits just to pay interest on the debt, let alone cover dividends. The market was understandably cautious. Debenhams tested the waters by saying the shares would be floated at somewhere between 195p and 250p.

It is quite normal for companies coming to market to indicate a prospective share price range. Initially this can be quite wide, though the margin is usually narrowed after the reaction of institutional investors is gauged.

Private investors do well to take note of where within the price range the shares are ultimately placed. It can be a good guide to how well the shares will subsequently perform. The higher up the range, the better the omens.

Figure 10.1: Debenhams

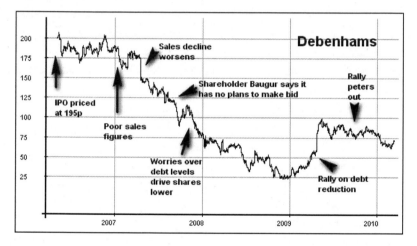

Debenhams shares were in fact floated through a book building exercise at 195p, right at the bottom of the range, which was a little surprising given that the company's advisers claimed the issue was more than twice subscribed – in other words, more than double the number of shares available could have been sold at that price.

The clear implication is that nearly all those applying for shares went in at 195p and were not prepared to pay more for the privilege. Applicants were probably influenced by the fact that Debenhams' stock market capitalisation was £1.6 billion while debt was not much less at £1.2 billion even after being reduced by £500 million from the proceeds of the flotation.

The shares immediately traded at 200p; within a couple of days they were at 205p.

So far so good.

However, those who chased after the shares in those very early days were soon showing a loss, and one that was doomed to endure long term despite a temporary pick up towards the year end.

In tough retail trading conditions, Debenhams was highly vulnerable so, when trading fell short of expectations during the key Christmas period in 2006, the shares fell back at the start of 2007.

Despite a brief recovery, a further worsening of sales figures sent the shares even lower. The chart was propped up for a time by hopes that Icelandic retailer Baugur would make a takeover offer – this was before the Icelandic financial system collapsed – but when Baugur ruled itself out and worries mounted over Debenhams' debt levels, the shares were in freefall.

They dipped momentarily beneath 25p, just one eighth of the float price, before a plan to reduce debt sparked a rally. Even then, Debenhams was forced to raise a further £323 million through placing an open offer to reduce debt in mid-2009.

Case study: New Look

After the strong rise in the UK stock market since March 2009, pundits were awaiting a flood of new issues in early 2010 to take advantage of rising share prices. The assumption was that one or two quite tasty dishes would be offered first to get the ball rolling. Instead we got New Look, whose emergence as front runner produced a lukewarm reaction.

It was particularly unfortunate to have a retailer owned by private equity coming to the fore. While four years is a long time in the stock market, few investors had forgotten the debacle of Debenhams.

It was mildly reassuring that the £650 million that New Look hoped to raise in equity would be used to pay down debt, although that would still leave an uncomfortable £450 million in borrowings.

Debts were so high because the private equity investors who took the business private in 2004 rewarded themselves by drawing cash out of the company.

New Look borrowed money for this payout in a PIK deal. PIK stands for payment in kind, which is a complete misnomer as it implies that the loan is paid off with goods rather than cash.

In fact, no payment of any description is made on a PIK loan. The interest is simply added on to borrowings, which snowball rapidly. The interest rate tends to be on the high side to compensate the lender for getting nothing back until the whole loan is repaid.

Thus a £359 million PIK loan had grown to something approaching £600 million in less than four years, about 15% per annum compound interest.

On the credit side, New Look had thrived under private ownership, with £450 million invested in the business. Sales were up and so was market share, helped by a policy of constantly renewing stock in the way that the Marks & Spencer franchise Per Una did in its heyday.

New Look also planned to open new stores to boost sales and, it hoped, profits – provided the already indebted company did not overstretch itself in the process.

Float falls flat

No doubt the company's private equity owners hoped that the dire shortage of new issues over the previous couple of years would send investors rushing to snap up New Look shares.

Two weeks later the proposed flotation was dropped with the advisers blaming the volatile market, a curious excuse given that the stock market was no longer seeing anything like the 100 points a day swings on the FTSE 100 index that had been commonplace in the previous year.

What actually happened was that large institutional investors were being justifiably cautious about who they were prepared to back. They were reluctant to commit themselves to New Look because of its higher level of debt, run up in part because its private equity backers had taken money out.

For New Look, the decision to pull the float must have been difficult. The longer the float was delayed, the more the expensive PIK loan would grow, thus making it increasingly difficult to attract investors.

Lessons learnt

- New issues may offer an opportunity to get in on the ground floor – if you are able to subscribe

- Some issues are restricted to institutional investors

- If you cannot invest in the float, let the shares settle before piling in

- Your chances of making a quick profit are pretty thin

- Beware companies that have been loaded up with debt by venture capitalist owners.

Chapter 11.
When Share Prices Fall

We all hope to buy on the cheap and sell at the top of the market, so it is natural to look for shares that have fallen heavily in the hope that they will rebound. Unfortunately it is quite likely that the shares will continue to fall after we have bought them.

It is particularly tempting to assume that well known names cannot possibly go under, an attitude that will have been strengthened by the bailing out of banks deemed too big to be allowed to go bust.

Yet big names have occasionally gone to the wall, including the last British motor giant, British Leyland. The banks survived only at the cost of seeing their share prices collapse and, in the case of Lloyds and Royal Bank of Scotland, with existing shareholders ending up owning a minority of shares and the Government taking control.

However, as long as we bear that caveat in mind and adopt a sensible, cautious approach, we will find that many ailing companies do eventually turn the corner. Sometimes, but not always, the signs are clear. Usually it is a case of sifting through the evidence and forming a judgement. Your attitude to risk will help to determine at what stage you will consider investing.

Questions to ask are:

- Are the markets in which the company operates still contracting?

- Has the company itself taken sufficient action such as reducing costs and cutting production?

- To what extent were the problems caused by poor management and how much was it down to a deterioration in the markets?

- Has the company gained or lost market share?
- If a dividend is still being paid, how well is it covered?
- Has new management been brought in?
- Are debt levels under control?

These questions can be asked if you are attempting to decide whether to get in before the crowd.

You do admittedly take the risk that conditions get worse rather than better but if you are satisfied that the company does have a long term future it should all come right in the long term.

However, if you still have doubts it will probably be better to hang on a little longer until you see more positive signs, which should emerge from questions like these:

- Have the markets the company operates in started to expand?
- Is the company starting to expand?
- Is there a new management team untainted by the mistakes of its predecessor?
- Have any profit warnings run their course?

A key issue in all this is how realistic management seems to be in owning up to the scale of any problems. Key tests include:

- Have pronouncements got progressively worse?
- Did any job losses come immediately or well after the crisis broke?
- Has cash flow been in or out? A company generating cash can survive through bad times for much longer
- If the dividend was reduced, was this done as soon as the company got into trouble?

We are naturally looking for decisive management: executives who spotted troubles early on and took evasive action where possible. We want a board that was upfront and truthful about the size and scope of the issues it faced.

Were the quarterly management statements clear in outlining the difficulties or were warnings hidden? If we are to believe that the corner has been turned we must be satisfied that we can trust what the company is telling us.

While it is incumbent on directors to put all issues that affect the share price into the public domain, they are only human. It is tempting to put the best gloss on the situation or to keep fingers crossed and hope to be rescued by divine providence.

Much of the fall in the stock markets at the turn of the millennium came because tech companies insisted that orders were being deferred, not lost, so investors were slow to realise that the dot.com bubble had burst. Punters who got their fingers badly burnt took a long time – about three years in fact – to trust company pronouncements again.

Case study: Wolseley

Problems may occur that are not directly of the company's making. Much of Wolseley's troubles came from expansion into the United States, a strategy that seemed solid enough through the early years of the new millennium and which contributed to continuing success. However, when the US housing market collapsed because banks had been lending to sub-prime borrowers, the strategy unravelled.

Builders' merchant Wolseley was once a high flier, a rare example of a thriving British company that successfully transferred its business model into Europe and across the Atlantic.

Wolseley concentrated on heating and plumbing, becoming well known in the UK for its specialist outlets such as Parts Center, Pipe Center and Drain Center.

There was much to commend about the way in which Wolseley expanded from modest beginnings. It grew by acquiring very small rivals and making a handful of Greenfield openings each year so that it was never overstretched. It had a specialist business but was not focused exclusively on one particular line of products, as it also provided construction materials.

It catered for the wholesale and the retail trade, for builders and do-it-yourself fans, for housing and commercial property.

As it expanded abroad, the chain freed itself from the vagaries of the UK market by diversifying gradually in other countries. It would take something pretty massive to shake the group to its foundations.

Alas, something massive did happen in the shape of the US sub-prime mortgage scandal and Wolseley's markets shrunk rapidly as the credit crunch hit the residential and commercial markets on both sides of the Atlantic.

It was pretty unusual for a company with a decent spread of products, geographic markets and types of customer to be hit right across the board but these were unusual times.

Figure 11.1: Wolseley

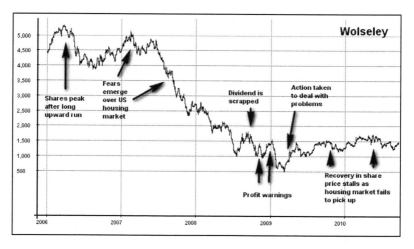

Wolseley's shares collapsed from a top side of £50 in early 2007 all the way down to £5 just 24 months later. There were four significant upward phases within this downward trend but these were clearly premature. Wolseley itself made no attempt to hide the fact that its markets continued to be difficult.

As late as September 2008, chief executive Chip Hornsby said bluntly:

> "When you look at the last 12 months, certainly the market conditions have been difficult, and unfortunately, are becoming even more difficult, particularly as you look at what's happened in the US and migrated now to Europe."

Hornsby was announcing a halving of operating profits from £753 million to £301 million in the 12 months to 31st July. Pre-tax profits had fallen even more heavily, by more than three quarters from £634 million to £145 million, and the final dividend was scrapped.

In fact it was a surprise in all the circumstances that the dividend had survived so long given the need to preserve cash. An interim dividend had been paid.

Indeed, one reason for being cautious about Wolseley was a feeling that management had been slow to react to the scope of the problem. It is true that not many people did foresee the whole capitalist system going to the brink of the abyss but you would have thought that Wolseley's US management would have had their ears to the ground in terms of that country's housing situation.

No doubt they preferred not to report back how bad things were. Investors should be aware that middle managers do not always face up to the scale of the problems.

The warning in September was underlined two months later, with quarterly figures showing a further fall in profits and a further warning that things were getting worse in the UK and Scandinavia.

There was still no reason to believe that Wolseley was over the worst, though some investors did buy in after the shares seemed to find solid support at £10. In early 2009, as the prognosis failed to improve, the shares plumbed new lows at 500p.

Getting to grips with problems

However, it was at this point that Wolseley finally came to grips with its problems. Firstly it proposed a placing and rights issue to raise £1 billion to reduce debt from £4.3 billion. At the same time it signed a two year debt agreement with five banks to put the group on a stable footing.

Secondly, Wolseley planned to cut back on poorly performing parts of the business and concentrate on the better prospects such as the core businesses in the UK, Ireland, Scandinavia and France, and plus plumbing and heating in North America, where it had sufficiently large operations giving good returns. Even so, no more cash was to be ploughed into expansion in France until the financial performance there improved.

A strategic review was to be launched into the Central and Eastern Europe business while the rest of the US business was to be sold or put into a joint venture. This was Stock, the second largest provider of building materials and construction services to professional home builders and contractors in the United States. It had proved particularly vulnerable to fluctuations in lumber prices.

Turning point

This was the stage at which the more adventurous investors could risk a punt. Wolseley did have a lot to prove but these were positive steps and a sign that problems had been identified and were being addressed.

It did in fact prove to be the turning point and the shares raced up to £15 before pausing for breath. This level had proved to be a ceiling right at the end of 2008 so it was perhaps no big surprise that the recovery ran out of steam. However, when the shares settled back to £10 there was good cause for even risk averse investors to join in.

Three times during the downward plunge the previous year, the shares had found buying support at this level so there was a good chance that they would fall no further. There were still considerable risks as markets continued to deteriorate but investors could feel that Hornsby was being entirely upfront with the bad news.

Furthermore, he was able to give specific figures about cost savings and details of measures taken to alleviate the situation.

Stock had been put into a joint venture and debt had been reduced to £1.5 billion, with unused overdraft facilities cancelled.

Hornsby warned that market conditions would not improve until the following year. Nonetheless the wider picture gave some grounds for hope. The world economic crisis showed signs of coming under control with meltdown avoided. Construction work, particularly in new homes, had been cut back so far that there was a backlog of work waiting to be released.

The shares did resume their upward path and, although they turned back twice at that troublesome £15 level in late 2009 and early 2010, they finally pushed higher.

Faith in Wolseley management to cope with the unprecedented difficulties was rewarded in May 2010 when the company was finally able to say that profits for the year to the end of the following July would beat analysts' expectations.

Catching falling knives

This is one of the most dangerous concepts in investing. It refers to shares that have fallen precipitately, to the point where (we hope) the only way is back up.

Catch the knife cleanly by the handle and you have a weapon to add to your armoury. However, you are more likely the grasp the blade and suffer a nasty cut.

It is true that the market tends to overdo its swings and then correct itself. Investors looking for a quick – and one must emphasise the word quick – profit *may* be able to get in and out if they get their timing right. This is the phenomenon known as a dead cat bounce, where a plunging share rebounds a little before resuming its fall.

Where a company's share price collapses we should bear in mind that:

- we are unlikely to see a dividend in the near future; companies with solid dividends do not crash

- apart from any short term upward blip, we are unlikely to see a substantial gain in the share price for a very long time

- existing shareholders could be wiped out in any recapitalisation.

One of the best examples of the phenomenon is Jarvis. One could say that Jarvis is two of the best examples – as lightning has struck the infrastructure provider twice.

Jarvis

Jarvis first ran into difficulties in May 2002 when the fatal train crash at Potters Bar in Hertfordshire occurred on a stretch of line maintained by Jarvis. The following year some local authority clients who had contracted Jarvis to build schools and work on other projects started to complain about the standard of work.

Jarvis was then subject to a TV documentary alleging that it was having difficulty in paying its subcontractors, who were refusing to take on more work until they were paid for what they had already done. It emerged that, in tendering for work at too cheap a price, Jarvis had committed itself to loss-making contracts.

In July 2004 Jarvis reported a loss of nearly £250 million for the year that had ended on 31st March and it admitted that the auditors had questioned whether the business was still a going concern. The auditors wondered whether Jarvis would recover money owed to it or whether further losses on contracts had been underestimated.

Four months later Jarvis admitted that it was using cash from selling off subsidiaries just to keep going rather than, as intended, to reduce debt.

You can't say you weren't warned! Yet some private investors bought into Jarvis as the shares crashed in the unjustifiable belief that the company would somehow survive. Super optimists bought shares even after Jarvis warned just before Christmas that it had enough money to last only to the end of January.

Far from recovering, Jarvis eventually wiped out its smaller shareholders and reduced larger shareholders to a combined total of just 5% of a reconstituted company.

Amazingly, history repeated itself in March 2010 when the reconstructed Jarvis called in the administrators after Network Rail cut its track renewal work by 30%. Again there were plenty of warning signs as work dried up and profits clumped before the shares were suspended at 9.4p.

Profit warnings

It is particularly foolhardy to snap up shares that have fallen after a surprise profit warning. This is unlikely to be the end of the bad news. Profit warnings, like London buses, tend to come along in threes.

Watch for companies that seem to be in denial over the extent of their problems. Very often there are warning signs for investors to pick up on within results and trading statements even if the company itself chooses to put the best gloss on matters.

Case study: Game Group

The situation looked highly discouraging in September 2009 when Game Group, a retailer of computer and video games, reported sales down 7% in the six months to the end of July despite the opening of more stores.

Although profit margins had improved, pre-tax profits slumped by two thirds from £32.8 million in the previous first half to £10.8 million.

In an upbeat statement, chairman Peter Lewis claimed these were solid results and he demonstrated his confidence by raising the interim dividend from 1.79p to 1.88p. His argument was that the previous year's figures had been boosted by 'unprecedented sales of hardware and record breaking software launches'.

Trading, he said, had returned to normal patterns 'where historically we have generated nearly all group profits in the second half of the year'.

Lewis was unfazed by the fact that sales in the 13 weeks to 19th September were down 8.8% overall and 16.6% on a like-for-like basis, which was even worse than the first half performance.

Less than two months later, with Game well into the crucial Christmas period, sales were reported to be down 11.3% over the previous 18 weeks, meaning that sales in the latest five years must have been well down on the previous year.

It was not until early January, after further falls in sales over Christmas, that Game admitted that profits would fall short of expectations. When the full year results came out in April, the chief executive quit and the chief operating officer in the UK also announced his departure in the face of a 28.7% fall in profits.

Figure 11.2: Game Group

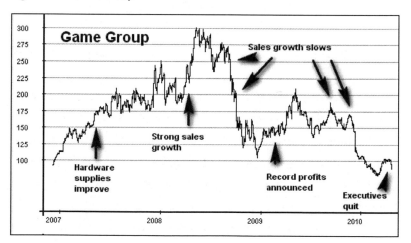

This was clearly a sudden development because no replacement had been lined up for the chief executive and a non-executive director had to step in on a temporary basis while Game scrabbled round for a suitable candidate.

Of greater concern was that sales had continued to fall, by more than 13%, after the financial year end.

What was instructive was the bullish tone of the announcements over this period. The fall in sales apparently was no reflection on the group itself: problems were always placed elsewhere.

Thus the sales fall was due to distortions in the release of new hardware and software and a difficult trading environment in which global sales fell by 20%. The statements in the meantime were littered with phrases such as 'we outperformed the market' or 'we remain optimistic' or 'strong balance sheet'.

Investors were not greatly impressed. The shares, which had peaked at 300p in the middle of 2008, were already falling heavily even before the chairman was protesting that the company was coping with problems. They halved from 250p before the half-year statement to 125p in mid-September.

Lessons learnt

- Share prices that have fallen offer opportunities for investors to buy in cheaply

- We must research such companies to see whether a fall has been overdone or whether investors are right to shun the shares

- Buying into companies that have seen their share price collapse is particularly dangerous. We could see our share holding wiped out.

Part III

Managing Your Portfolio

Chapter 12.
Monitoring Your Portfolio

As we build up our portfolio we should monitor how well our existing holdings are faring, rather than simply bury our heads in the sand and hope for the best. We want to know whether we are on the right track before we commit ourselves further.

To start, keep a record of each purchase with the name of the company, number of shares bought and price paid. You should also record any dividends received.

You can do this on good old-fashioned paper, although it will be rather laborious as you will have to manually check the current share price and calculate profit or loss on each investment. More convenient is a spreadsheet (e.g. Excel) which can be set up to calculate your profits so far, although you will still have to manually input most of the data.

An alternative is to use a software program, such as Sharescope (**www.ionic.co.uk**), which is designed for building and monitoring portfolios. These programs are usually installed on your computer with current share price data downloaded over the internet.

If you invest online with a broker, the broker's own website will usually have a portfolio feature that records your purchases, displays current prices and calculates your profits and losses to date.

Another alternative would be to use the portfolio functionality that is offered by many websites, such as, ADVFN, Yahoo, Digital Look or Motley Fool. With such services, you input details on the shares you've bought and their valuation is automatically updated by the website.

Here is a sample portfolio on a Motley Fool ISA account. Each trade made is automatically added to the portfolio. The table is very easy to understand.

Figure 12.1: Sample screenshot of an online portfolio

Personal reference:			Cash in account:	£ 10.00
Account code:			Left to subscribe in this tax year:	£ 8,261.50
Account status:		Okay to trade	Dividend Option:	Pay Away Immediately

Printer Friendly View

Company Name	Listed on Market	Quantity	Avg Cost Per Share (p) *	Latest Price (p) **	Change (p)	Book Cost (£)	Valuation (£)	Profit/Loss £	Profit/Loss %			
ATK	LSE	150	612.94	710.00	97.06	919.41	1,065.00	145.59	15.84	£+	£-	⊞
BBY	LSE	400	271.995	271.90	-0.10	1,087.98	1,087.60	-0.38	-0.03	£+	£-	⊞
BDEV	LSE	900	113.6156	70.05	-43.57	1,022.54	630.45	-392.09	-38.34	£+	£-	⊞
HRN	LSE	700	150.57	155.00	4.43	1,053.99	1,085.00	31.01	2.94	£+	£-	⊞
JMAT	LSE	70	1,517.5286	1,804.00	286.47	1,062.27	1,262.80	200.53	18.88	£+	£-	⊞
NG.	LSE	210	549.4095	572.00	22.59	1,153.76	1,201.20	47.44	4.11	£+	£-	⊞
RDSB	LSE	60	1,723.55	1,924.00	200.45	1,034.13	1,154.40	120.27	11.63	£+	£-	⊞
SBRY	LSE	300	325.20	357.90	32.70	975.60	1,073.70	98.10	10.06	£+	£-	⊞
SFR	LSE	500	208.026	255.00	46.97	1,040.13	1,275.00	234.87	22.58	£+	£-	⊞
SDY	LSE	4000	30.8108	28.25	-2.56	1,232.43	1,130.00	-102.43	-8.31	£+	£-	⊞
TW.	LSE	2500	39.4624	24.39	-15.07	986.56	609.75	-376.81	-38.19	£+	£-	⊞
						Total	**£11,574.90**	**£6.10**	**0.05%**			

The top right hand corner tells us how much cash is in the account (£10) and whether dividends are reinvested automatically, held in the account or paid to the holder's bank account. As this is an ISA account there is a limit to how much can be invested each year. The remaining amount that can be invested in the current financial year is shown.

The companies in the ISA account are listed down the left hand side. You can click on any symbol to find the full name of the company and the dealing record in those shares.

Other columns provide details of the number of shares held, what we paid per share and in total, what the holdings are currently worth and how much profit or loss each share has produced. At the bottom we see our total gain/loss so far.

As dividends are paid direct to this particular holder's account, the screen does not show total returns. You would have to keep a record of dividends paid and add these to the change in share values to get a full picture. If you reinvest your dividends or retain them in the account, these will be included in your total.

It is also possible to monitor portfolios on portable devices such as mobile phones, although these are likely to be of more use to traders than investors.

As always in investing, do it the way that suits you.

With the current computer and online services that exist it may seem a little perverse to record portfolio transactions on paper. However, one could argue that fewer mistakes are made when you diligently record trades on paper; and paper rarely has problems of freezing up or requiring upgrades.

How often to monitor

When we first buy shares we may well find we look at their current price several times a day; but then our checks become less frequent as the novelty wears off.

There is no set frequency for checking your portfolio. The more actively you trade, the more often you need to check up on your performance. Those investing for capital gains will be more assiduous than dividend seekers, since they will be on the lookout for buying and selling opportunities.

It makes sense to do a quick check once a day, preferably soon after the market has opened, so you can spot any reaction to the day's announcements issued at 7 am, or after the market has closed so you can see how your shares have moved during the day's trading.

It is unwise not to monitor your portfolio at least once a week. A lot can happen over five trading days.

Measuring performance

Using a benchmark

It is very tempting to measure success in terms of whether or not we have made a profit, but a more sophisticated approach is to consider whether we have beaten the market overall. If our portfolio has increased by 12% over a certain period we may feel pleased with our stock-picking abilities; but if, over the same period, the stock market has risen by 19%, should we still feel so smug?

We need a benchmark to measure our performance against.

The simplest benchmark is what would have happened if we had not bought shares and just left our money in, say, a simple savings account. Have our shares, plus dividends received, beaten what we would have earned in interest? That is surely the minimum we would wish for.

Beyond that, we need a benchmark for the stock market.

FTSE (a joint-venture between the *Financial Times* and the London Stock Exchange) produce a range of indices that can act as useful benchmarks for stock market performance.

A stock market index is a way of calculating the average performance of a collection of shares – for example, the FTSE 100 Index measures the average performance of 100 UK companies. Different indices exist to measure the performance of different collections of shares.

A brief description of the major FTSE UK indices is given in the accompanying box.

FTSE indices

FT Ordinary Share Index (FT30)

The FT30 Index was introduced in 1935 by the *Financial Times* and calculated from a subjective collection of 30 major companies – which in the early years were concentrated in the industrial and retailing sectors. For a long time the Index was the best known performance measure of the UK stock market. But the index become less representative of the whole market and so the FT30 has been usurped by the FTSE 100.

FTSE 100

Today, the FTSE 100 Index (sometimes called the "Footsie") is the most well known index tracking the performance of the UK stock market. The index comprises 100 of the largest stocks listed on the LSE, and represents approximately 80% of the total market (by capitalisation).

FTSE 250

Similar in construction to the FTSE 100, except it comprises the next 250 largest stocks listed on the LSE after the top 100. The index is sometimes referred to as the index of mid-cap stocks, and comprises approximately 18% of the total market capitalisation.

FTSE 350

Similar in construction to the FTSE 100, but including all the companies from the FTSE 100 and FTSE 250 indices.

FTSE Small Cap

Comprised of companies with a market capitalisation below the FTSE 350 and represents about 2% of the total market by capitalisation.

FTSE All-Share

The FTSE All-Share is the aggregation of the FTSE 100, FTSE 250 and FTSE Small Cap indices.

When measuring a portfolio against a benchmark, it is important to compare like with like. For example, if a portfolio is comprised mainly of large UK companies then the obvious benchmark would be the FTSE 100 Index, but for a portfolio of small companies the FTSE Small-Cap Index may be more appropriate.

Let's look at an example.

The following chart shows the performance of Euromoney shares compared to the FTSE 100 Index for the period 2003-2006.

Figure 12.2: Euromoney v FTSE 100 Index (2003-2006)

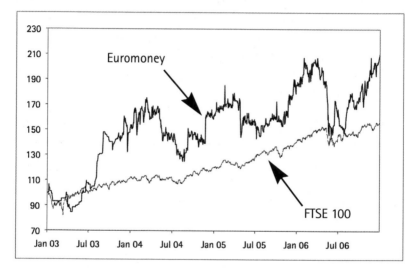

An investor holding Euromoney shares over this period may have felt pleased with his superior stock-picking skills – the shares mainly outperformed the index.

However, Euromoney is a mid-cap stock and is in the FTSE 250 Index (not the FTSE 100 Index of large-cap stocks), so let's add the FTSE 250 Index to the chart.

Figure 12.3: Euromoney v FTSE 100 Index v FTSE 250 (2003-2006)

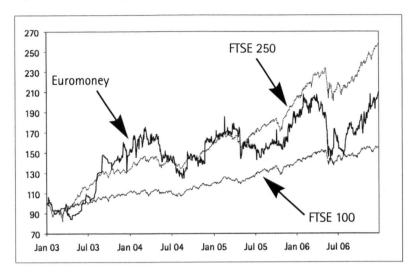

As can be seen, Euromoney shares performed largely in line with the FTSE 250 Index for a couple of years and then significantly under-performed.

Over the period 2003-2006 mid-cap stocks greatly outperformed large cap stocks so, judging Euromoney against the more appropriate FTSE 250 Index, its performance could be seen as disappointing.

Having said that, the usual benchmark that most investors use (rightly or wrongly) is the FTSE 100.

If we can beat the performance of the FTSE 100 Index we have done better than putting our cash into a simple tracker fund.

One obvious difficulty is the time frame. Unless we invest our entire portfolio at one go, we will be holding our shares over different periods. To be fully accurate we should measure the performance of each share separately against the index for the relevant period but that is rather cumbersome and time consuming.

Each time you buy or sell a share, note the level of the index at that point, and your outperformance or underperformance at that point, and start measuring again.

Benefits of monitoring

There are two major benefits of monitoring the performance of your portfolio:

1. You notice which shares are underperforming and which have overperformed

2. You can see if your portfolio is becoming unbalanced.

If one component of your portfolio has fared poorly you need to assess whether you made the wrong choice – decide whether there were factors that you overlooked and whether it is time to admit your mistake and cut your losses.

If a share has done particularly well, consider whether it is time to cash in and switch into something else. If you are investing for capital gains you will be more inclined to take your profit; dividend seekers will be more inclined to hold unless the yield has shrunk to the point where you can do better elsewhere.

Take your decision calmly and without sentiment. These are only shares, not best friends that you are considering dumping. Before you cash in, ask yourself where you are going to park the cash. There is no point in selling your shares unless there is a better prospect elsewhere.

Inevitably some of your investments will do better than others. Sometimes the gap between best and worst performers will be stark. Anyone who invested in just a couple of tech stocks around 1998 would have found themselves heavily overloaded in that sector by early 2000; anyone buying a couple of tech stocks in 2000 would have found that technology occupied a tiny percentage of the value of the portfolio by the time the market hit the bottom in March 2003.

Consider this balanced portfolio of five stocks from different sectors set up at the start of 2009 with roughly £10,000 invested in each. One share tripled in value and two others more than doubled while one fell back heavily, so that within just 18 months the portfolio was unbalanced.

Company	Start Jan 2009	Shares bought	End June 2010	Value at end	% of portfolio
Latchways	400p	2,500	665p	£16,625	16.0
Domino Printing	206p	4,850	455p	£22,067	21.2
Cairn Energy	202p	4,950	415p	£20,542	19.8
Weir	310p	3,220	1050p	£33,810	32.5
Lloyds	85p	11,760	54p	£10,878	10.5

From having five shares occupying one fifth each, we now have one share representing almost a third of our portfolio while another is only a tenth. The problem is that we no longer have a well-diversified portfolio – instead we have a portfolio whose value will be disproportionately affected by the movements of one company (Weir).

If our portfolio becomes unbalanced we have three choices:

1. Do nothing and carry on regardless

2. Sell part or all of our holding in the overweight share or sector and invest in a different sector where we are underweight

3. Buy more shares in sectors where we are underweight.

Doing nothing is an option if your portfolio is not seriously unbalanced. After all, if a share has done well you should discard it with reluctance as it may continue its upward run. City professionals will often recommend being overweight in a particular stock or sector with good prospects.

There is no set rule for how far out of line you can go without getting concerned. I would suggest that if any one share or sector becomes more than one third of your portfolio you are putting yourself too much at the mercy of the elements.

Selling part of your holding to scale down an overweight stock makes a lot of sense. You retain a stake in a company that has done well for you but take some profit to spread your portfolio.

If we have more cash to invest we may be able to rebalance the portfolio through new share purchases. This will certainly be the case in the early stages of building a portfolio where we are seeking to diversify anyway.

Chapter 13.
Stop Losses and Averaging Down

Stop losses

Many investors believe that every portfolio should operate a stop loss system. The basic principle is that if you buy shares in a company and the shares fall in price then you have a system in place that sells the shares for you automatically after they've fallen to a certain price.

There is much to commend this approach. The hardest thing for any investor, even City professionals, is to admit that you made a mistake. At least if you get out quickly before too much damage is done, you live to invest another day.

If you choose to limit your losses you need to decide how far the shares have to fall before you take action: 5%? 10%? 15%?

There is unfortunately no definitive answer. If you sell out at the smallest setback then you may be panicking over what turns out to be a minor blip. If you hang on too long you may find yourself nursing a nasty loss, the very event that you were trying to avoid.

Even with an automatic stop loss sell programme you may be unable to get out at your chosen price if the shares fall sharply.

This is particularly true if a share price falls heavily at the opening of trading in the morning. Shares do not necessarily open at the same price as they closed the previous evening, especially if price sensitive news such as company results or a trading statement is released at the usual time of 7 am.

Table 13.1: Comparison of closing and opening prices (gapping)

Company	Close 6/9/10	Open 7/9/10	Reason for change
Redrow	135.25p	133.25p	Profit taking after 40% rise
Rio Tinto	3620p	3646p	Invests in diamond mine
Town Centre Secs	139p	150p	Results
Just Car Clinics	49.5p	51.5p	Results
Logica	119p	122.75p	No obvious reason

The table shows the difference in the closing price and the following day's opening price of a selection of stocks taken at random on a day when share prices were generally little changed at the opening.

Retaining flexibility

There is also the question of whether you are going to pay your stockbroker to operate the stop loss for you automatically or monitor the performance of your shares yourself.

An automatic programme does prevent you from shilly-shallying if a share you were particularly fond of turns into one of life's disappointments. On the other hand it removes flexibility. When a share price falls you should take another look to decide whether the downturn is justified – perhaps you had overlooked factors that more savvy investors had spotted – or whether a recovery is a reasonable prospect.

The longer your timeframe, the less important a stop loss is, though even long term investors should investigate further if a constituent of their portfolio performs badly. When you are looking to turn a quick profit it is vital to clear out the dead wood promptly. If you are looking for a long term gain or investing for income, you can afford to ride out the short term dips that beset even the best of companies from time to time.

Special situations

Beware, also, of artificial dips in a share price that could spark a stop loss sale unnecessarily. This could happen if:

1. the shares go ex-dividend

2. a rights issue is announced

3. a proposed takeover bid stalls.

We will take a brief look at each of these cases.

1. Going ex-dividend

When a dividend is paid, the shares tend to fall by the amount of the dividend. Unless this is a particularly high yielding stock, such a fall is unlikely to be large enough to spark a stop loss but, if the stock market is down overall that day, the combined effect could tip the balance.

You need to decide whether, having collected the dividend, you want to stay in for another six months round to the next payout or cash in. This is a conscious decision for you to take in the light of the facts, not something that an automatic trading programme dictates.

2. Rights issues

Rights issues normally push shares lower. That is because investors are being asked to pump in more money and they need to be tempted by being offered shares at below the prevailing stock market price.

The shares will tend to fall to a price somewhere between the stock market price and the rights issue price, depending on the size of the issue and the size of the discount. Such a fall could very easily spark a stop loss, especially if the rights issue is a hefty one.

You may indeed wish to sell your holding if you do not want to invest more money in the company. However, this is a decision for you to take in the circumstances and not a cause to sell out because some computer programme doesn't like it.

You need to consider whether, in fact, you wish to take advantage of the offer to top up your holdings at a cheaper price.

We look at this issue in a later chapter.

3. Bid situations

If you hold shares in a company that is the subject of a takeover bid, you should abandon all thoughts of operating a stop loss and concentrate on the circumstances of the bid.

You would normally expect the bid to be at a premium to the previous stock market price and that the shares will rise immediately to reflect the value of the offer. However, if there are doubts about the bid – for example, it may be conditional on various factors including due diligence – the shares may well drift.

Likewise, a second bidder showing interest will push the shares above the value of the existing offer. If the second bidder subsequently seems to be getting cold feet, the shares will fall back. Although you have missed the best opportunity to get out, you may want to see the battle through to the end.

Takeovers are covered in a later chapter.

Humans before robots

The point is that there are always investment decisions to be made and these depend on human judgement, not the actions of a robot.

Many investors swear by stop losses and will point to occasions where they saved money during a share downturn, either in the market as a whole or for a particular share that they held. Such evidence will spring readily to their minds. Less obvious will be the times that they lost out by selling into a temporary dip. As they move on to other investments they may not notice that the shares they dumped bounced back.

Protagonists of stop loss programmes argue that they limit losses. Critics argue that they guarantee losses – you are specifically choosing to sell at a loss and you have incurred two lots of dealing fees in buying and selling.

Flash crash

The events of 6th May 2010 were admittedly extreme but they provide an object lesson on the dangers of stop loss orders.

Stock markets around the world crashed on fears over debts in the Eurozone, brought to a head by the real possibility that one euro member, Greece, would default on its debts and that this would cause a domino effect in other highly indebted countries such as Portugal, Spain and Italy. The whole future of the euro as a single currency was at stake.

Now it was perfectly reasonable to take fright at the events of that week and to decide that the markets would fall further. Such a decision would have been based on a rational assessment of the markets. It would, in the event, have been wrong, for markets bounced back very quickly and you would have sold at the bottom. But that's life.

Other investors took the rational decision that the fears were overdone and that the markets would recover. They gambled on there being sufficient determination within the European Union to sort out the mess, rescue the ailing economies and impose greater financial discipline on them.

It is easy with hindsight to know which camp was right. The point is that those who took a considered view of the situation stood a chance. They were able to assess whether the market was down on purely short term technical factors on an unduly volatile day.

Those who blindly sold because they had an automatic stop loss were not in a position to choose their course of action. What were temporary losses for many investors turned into real losses for the unlucky people with stop losses.

If you are a long term investor it is best not to get bogged down in straight jacket rules that dictate when you buy and sell. Using stop losses makes far more sense for short term investors who rely on the momentum of the market for a quick turnaround and who cannot risk letting the market turn even more against them.

Even professional investors have difficulty in gauging how long or how far market trends will go and where the turning point will be. Smaller investors who do not have sophisticated trading systems will have greater difficulty in playing a short term game.

Dangers of set formulae

It must be stressed that stop losses do impose a sense of discipline but they are usually a formula for poor investing results because they encourage investors to sell low. When combined with any formula that leads investors to buy high – such as, for example, only buying shares in the top 25% of their peer groups – they are a recipe for disaster.

Using a set formula implies that you do not have the strength of your own convictions. If you have done your homework researching the fundamentals of a stock and nothing intrinsic has changed since then, you should consider whether to buy more stock when the price is going down – with the big proviso that you really are satisfied that nothing has changed. Do be prepared in these circumstances to consider whether you have overlooked something crucial.

Perhaps more importantly, if you feel the need to use artificial selling rules to protect yourself from big losses, it could be a sign of a mismatch between your asset allocation and your time horizon. If you are holding stocks in an account where you can't afford to lose much money, you're in the wrong asset class. Stop loss orders are not the answer.

Employing a stop loss strategy sounds appealing to an investor who is averse to risk but who cannot actively monitor his or her portfolio. In the case of a traditional stop loss order, once the stop price is reached, a market order to sell the security is entered by the investor's broker, assuming the broker is willing to do this.

Otherwise the investor must watch the share price movement of the entire portfolio, which rather defeats the object of not becoming absorbed in the holdings.

Hence, the trade will normally be made at or near the predetermined stop price – but not necessarily so. As was the case in the 'flash crash' market in early May 2010, if there is insufficient liquidity or the market is moving quickly, there is a good chance that the order could be filled at an even less favourable price. Thus the loss will be greater than the 10% stop loss anyway.

If you hold a stock with a stop loss of 10%, the only thing you are guaranteeing is that you will lose 10% on that trade if the shares fall, even if the setback is only temporary. Critics say that a more appropriate name for stop loss order would be guaranteed loss order.

Moving stop loss

If, as you hope, your shares perform well, the concept of a stop loss soon loses its immediacy. Say you set the stop loss at 10% but, instead of falling as you feared, your shares rise 10%.

That is great news but what protection do you have if the shares suddenly fall back again? They could tumble by 20% before hitting your stop loss and now you will be nursing a loss instead of those lovely gains.

The way round this is to keep moving your stop loss up in line with the share price so that the stop loss is never more than 10% (or whatever percentage you have chosen to set) below the prevailing stock market share price.

You raise the stop loss when the shares go up but never lower it if the shares fall as that would defeat the object of the exercise. If the shares fall below this moving line then you sell, but in this case you are at least cashing in a profit.

As with the initial stop loss, the disadvantage is that you may be forced out by a temporary blip and miss the opportunity of considerable further gains if the shares start to rise again, as they may well do. Remember that trends in share prices tend to continue for longer than you expect, so a rise in the share price is likely to be resumed.

The big advantage is that the shares may be peaking after a long run and could fall back quite sharply. At least with a moving stop loss you preserve most of your gains.

Averaging down

In stark contrast to running a stop loss is the concept of averaging down the price at which you bought shares. The idea is that if shares that you bought fall, then instead of getting out you buy more shares at the lower price.

This is how it works.

Say you buy shares at 100p and they fall to 80p. You need them to return all the way to 100p to break even.

So you buy the same number of shares at 80p, making the average price 90p a share. Thus if the shares recover to 90p you are breaking even again, and should they climb back to the original price of 100p you are showing a profit.

This argument has certain flaws. It is true that if you have twice as many shares then you make twice the gains if they go up in price. But what if they continue to fall, as may well happen? You are now losing money twice as fast.

If you thought the shares were such a great prospect, why did you not buy more in the first place? You should be thanking your lucky stars that you didn't. Perhaps you did not want to overweight your portfolio in a particular sector or maybe you had committed as much cash to your shares portfolio as you were comfortable with. Why overextend yourself chasing after a company that has, so far, let you down?

Averaging down encourages you to refuse to face up to the fact that you may have got it wrong. If you do decide to buy at the lower level you would do better to consider this as two separate investments. You should look again at the company, what it does, how it is performing and, what its prospects are, and then do the same for the sector it operates in.

You should particularly try to find what it was that you missed first time round. If, after all that, you feel that the shares represent even better value now than when you first bought, all well and good. By all means back your judgement. Just don't try to kid yourself.

Case study: Hornby

Let us suppose we decided to buy shares in toy maker Hornby late in 2009.

There were sound reasons to do so. The shares had fallen from 300p a year earlier to a low of 60p before recovering along with the rest of the stock market in 2009. After struggling to break above resistance at 150p, the shares finally broke higher and it looked to be time to get on the bandwagon.

Surely the upward surge had been resumed, so we bought 1000 shares at 170p, a total cost of £1700 plus the dealing charge.

Figure 13.1: Hornby

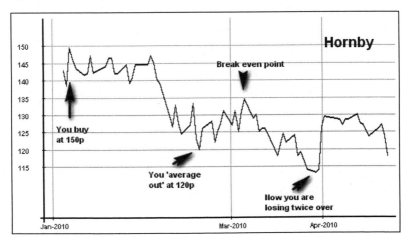

Alas, this proved to be a false signal and the shares sank back over the next few months, producing a loss on our investment of about £500. Never mind, on 18th February 2010 the shares stood at 120p and here was a chance to average out the price of our purchase. By buying another 1000 shares at a buying price of 122p, total cost of £1220, we now have 2000 shares that cost us a total of £2920.

This looked a pretty shrewd move on 5th March when the shares had recovered to 134.5p. Our total holding was now worth nearly £2700, with our overall loss reduced to about £250 allowing for dealing costs and the spread between the buying and selling price.

This was a chance to cut our losses and get out but, human nature being what it is, we probably decided to stay in until we had recovered all our losses.

By 16th March Hornby shares languished at 118p. We now had a small loss on the second purchase to add to the much larger loss on the first tranche of shares.

In fact, Hornby was a risky investment and while there was a fair case for taking a gamble (provided we were happy with risk and could afford to stand a loss) there were warning signs telling us not to overextend ourselves.

The last set of interim results, to the previous 30th September, had shown profits down by more than half from £1.8 million to £740,000 and the interim dividend had been scrapped.

The latest trading statement, covering the important Christmas period, showed trading was in line with expectations, which was all very well, but expectations were for full year profits to be down from £6.5 million to £5 million. That meant second half profits would be lower than in the previous second half, down from £4.7 million to £4.2 million.

This would be the second consecutive year of falling profits as the recession took its toll on leisure spending.

Our investment decision should have been based on these factors, not on some mathematical sleight of hand.

Lessons learnt

- Ask yourself whether you are right to continue investing in a company before you make each subsequent purchase

- Treat every purchase as a separate investment

- Trying to average out the cost of buying shares in a particular company can be a pointless distraction

- Face facts if you have made a poor investment rather than trying to salvage something from the mess.

Chapter 14.
Adding to Existing Holdings

Distinct from the mechanical process of pound cost averaging, we may decide to make fresh purchases of shares in companies that we have already invested in.

This will be because:

- we already have at least ten companies in our portfolio to give a wide spread of risk

- we have a sufficient variety of sectors in our portfolio

- we are not concerned about adding to the weighting of the company or sector we are proposing to invest in

- we believe that the company's shares still represent good value.

It does make a lot of sense to follow up success in a company that you already know rather than use the same money to take a speculative stake in a company that you are less familiar with.

You would normally add to an existing share holding in a company by buying in the stock market at the prevailing share price, just as you bought in the first place. (We shall look in a later chapter at situations where we have the chance to buy more shares because of corporate action.)

Adding to existing holdings has a number of advantages:

- You buy when you choose to

- You buy when you have spare cash to invest

- You buy when you feel the market is right

- You choose which company you want to increase your investment in

- You buy when you feel the share price is right

- You choose how many extra shares to buy or how much more cash to put in.

You are in complete control. You do not need to add to your holdings if you do not have the available cash or you feel you have sufficient exposure in the market or in a particular sector.

One of the shares you hold may look attractive but perhaps you feel that the current market price is a little on the top side. You can watch how the shares perform and see if the price falls to the level at which you feel comfortable in increasing your exposure.

Above all you choose which company you invest in further. You pick the one whose share price looks cheapest, offers the highest yield or is in a growing market.

Changes in circumstances

It is very important, when you make this decision, that you do so rationally on the basis of prevailing circumstances. This is a separate decision from your original choice to invest in this particular company.

The share price is unlikely to be the same as you paid originally. You also need to decide whether you want to buy the same number of shares again, fewer, or more. Remember, if the share price has gone up you will get fewer shares for the same amount of money; if it has gone down you will get more shares.

Another consideration is how many companies you have in your portfolio. The fewer companies you have invested in, the more sensible it is that you should look for a new investment rather than put even more of your eggs into too few baskets.

Likewise if your investments are mainly in one sector you should be thinking about diversifying into new areas rather than concentrating further on your pet project. Spreading risk means you will not take so much of a blow if circumstances turn against your favourite sector.

On the other hand, if you have a dozen shares in your portfolio and feel that this is quite a large enough number of companies to keep tabs on it makes sense to add to what you already have.

Your decision will be influenced by factors such as:

- Will adding to my holding unbalance my portfolio? Will I be concentrating too heavily on one particular share or sector?

- What has the company said about its prospects since my original investment? Do any such pronouncements make me feel more confident that I am on the right track or do they add a note of caution?

- Has the share price gone up since I last bought? Does that make the shares too expensive or do I feel that there is further to go? Good news from the company may have justified a higher rating.

- Has the share price gone down? Does this mean that the shares are even more of a bargain or is it a warning sign that the market has spotted something you have overlooked?

Your additional investment should also be seen within the context of the wider stock market. Is now a good time to be buying?

Just because you have already bought a range of shares and you now have more spare cash to invest, it does not mean you should pile in willy nilly. Take a look at how the stock market has performed of late.

Are market indices rising or falling? Are they bouncing around erratically? Are there economic factors buoying up or weighing down on shares?

During the dot.com bust at the start of the millennium, or the sub-prime mortgage crisis of 2007-9, it was wise to hold back from making a further commitment until markets settled. However, when it became clear in both cases that markets had hit the bottom and were recovering lost ground, there was a strong case for joining in the fun.

The wider picture is not the be all and end all. During any bull market some companies still run into trouble; any bear market produces well run companies that defy the downward trend. However, it is worth remembering that investments are not made in isolation. We are all part of a global economy.

Lessons learnt

- Adding to existing holdings makes sense if we can cash in on a success story at a company we are already familiar with

- It may be best to stick with companies already in your portfolio if it is broadly based

- Treat each purchase as a separate investment that needs to be justified

- Beware of unbalancing your portfolio with extra purchases.

Chapter 15.
Selling Existing Holdings

The time will inevitably come when we decide to sell some or all of our shares. The reason for selling might be:

1. We need cash urgently and cannot raise it elsewhere

2. We have lost faith in one of the companies we have invested in

3. Shares in one of our investments have shot up and we want to take profits

4. One of our investments is the subject of a takeover bid and we wish to cash in

5. The whole stockmarket looks overpriced and we are fearful of a sharp correction.

We will briefly look at each of these situations in turn.

1. Cash needed

This is the very situation we try to avoid by leaving enough cash on hand to cover emergencies. It is important, however great the panic, to take a calm, collected decision on what shares to sell. The upside of this situation is that it imposes some discipline, as we are forced to make a full assessment of our portfolio.

Assuming we are not so desperate that we need to sell the whole portfolio, common sense should prevail. We should aim to sell those shares offering the lowest yields or the fewest prospects of a rise in the share price.

Bear in mind the time frame you have for your investments. If you tend to hold shares for the long term you may, for example, decide to hold on to a company with a depressed share price that offers good prospects of recovery next year.

Since we are enforced sellers, we do not wish to sell more shares than we need to. It may be possible to sell only part of our holding in a company that we would prefer to retain if that raises enough to get by.

Three other considerations may affect our decision.

Firstly, selling a large holding may incur a capital gain. Unless you feel strongly that this company must go, it may be better to part with a holding in another company where your profits are not so great. After all, you are trying to raise a requisite amount of cash rather than crystallise a profit.

It may be possible, if you are facing a financial crisis in February or March, to split the sale into two tranches, selling the first batch in one financial year and the second in the next financial year starting on 6th April, and thus make use of two capital gains allowances.

You may also be able to consider selling a loss-making holding alongside a profitable one, so that the capital loss partly offsets the capital gain to the extent that your overall gain is pulled below the threshold.

Secondly, one company in your portfolio may be the subject of takeover rumours or an actual bid. The risk of a share price fall if the bid comes to nothing is correspondingly greater and you should consider making this your enforced sale.

Thirdly, if we are selling a particularly large block of shares it may not be possible to sell our entire holding in one batch. Each company has what is called a normal market size (usually abbreviated to NMS) which itself depends on the size of the company and how liquid the trading is in its shares. The NMS is likely to be 1000, 2000 or 5000 shares and, as the name suggests, the figure represents the normal size of each sale/purchase of these shares.

2. Lost faith in the company

This eliminates the need to agonise over which shares to sell. It is important that we should face reality if a company we selected has fallen short of expectations. Even professional investors find it hard to admit when they are wrong.

Bear in mind that investors tend to be reluctant to cut losses and only too ready to take profits, arguing that a profit is a profit is a profit. It is worth reiterating that trends in share prices tend to continue for longer than you expect, so a share price that has fallen is likely to fall further while a rising star will probably keep rising.

If your reason for investing is to secure dividends, then your criteria for getting out or staying in are different. Your prime consideration is whether the dividend is at risk from some previously unforeseen event or a profit warning.

You do not have to sell your entire holding. Say you sell half of your stake and retain the other half. This way, if the shares go up, you still enjoy some profit whereas if the shares fall you have averted a complete disaster.

Selling part of a shareholding is a highly contentious area of investing. It smacks of dithering. Do you want to get out of this company or not? And what proportion of your holding do you sell? Half and half seems a fair compromise but why not a quarter or three quarters or any other proportion? There is simply no satisfactory answer to this question.

Another important issue is what you intend to do with the money you raise from the share sale. Unless you need the cash you are presumably going to reinvest the proceeds. So before you sell shares in one company you need to select one that offers better prospects. Otherwise you may be jumping out of the frying pan into the fire.

3. Taking profits

This raises similar issues, although in this case we are entitled to feel a little smug. Haven't we done well! Remember that market trends tend to continue so the gains may have still further to run.

As always, take a cold, rational decision. Do not act on a sentimental attachment to a company that has done well for you in the past. Your judgement should be based on prospects for the future and whether you can switch into an even better investment.

It is particularly tempting to sell only part of your holding when you are nursing a healthy profit. You can sell enough shares to cover your original investment. The remaining holding has effectively cost you nothing so you are gambling with free chips. If the shares do fall back you cannot suffer an overall loss; if they continue to rise you make further profits.

It may also be sensible to sell your holding in two batches if you can split a capital gain between two tax years to avoid a tax liability.

4. Stockmarket is overpriced

This is an issue for your whole portfolio and not just one component.

It is time to reassess your strategy and your entire portfolio. Your decisions will be affected, at least in part, by whether you are looking for capital gains or income.

If your raison d'être is to buy and sell at a profit then fears of an economic downturn will prompt you to consider a wholesale clearout. Even so, you should assess each company individually. In any bear market some companies see their share prices rise so do not sell for the sake of it

Decide which companies in your portfolio are most vulnerable to a downturn and sell those first.

If the market moves lower, you have got rid of the dross before it is too late. You can now reassess whether your first instinct was right and the market has further to fall, in which case you can continue selling, or whether the fall has gone far enough and you can hang on to the better parts of your portfolio after all.

If the market rises you have kept the most promising shares and can reassess whether you were wrong to fear a fall in the market or whether the blip offers a better chance to sell out.

Case study: Warren Buffett and Kraft

A high profile example of putting your shares where your mouth is was Warren Buffett and Kraft. The famous investor held an 8.8% stake in the US food group when it launched a takeover bid for Cadbury, the chocolates, chewing gum and soft drinks company.

While many people in the UK (though not the happy Cadbury shareholders) were complaining about the acquisition by a foreign company of one of our best known brands, Buffett had a contrary grouse: he was convinced that Kraft was overpaying and to make matters worse Kraft sold valuable, profitable assets to help pay for the deal.

Although he has a lot of clout, not even Buffett could derail the takeover but he did not have to stick around with management he had so roundly criticised on several occasions during the bid period.

Through his Berkshire Hathaway investment vehicle he sold more than a quarter of his stake in Kraft over a period of weeks, reducing his holding to 6.1%. Because he held such a large stake, Buffett could not part with it in one batch. That is not such a problem for modest private investors who usually have the option of dumping shares rapidly without driving the share price substantially lower.

Keeping calm

You cannot hope to spot every looming disaster and if bad news hits the shares of one of your holdings the market will react faster than you can. You will thus be faced with taking the unpleasant decision of whether to cling on in the hope of recovery or get out at a lower price.

This is a decision that you must take in a calm and collected way, looking at the available evidence without any feelings of sentiment towards the company concerned. Bad news tends to be followed by more bad news so your instinct should be to err on the side of cutting your losses (or, we would hope, taking your profits).

If you do decide to hang on you must watch the shares on a daily basis until you are satisfied that the crisis is over.

It is rare indeed for a share to fall from hero to zero in one trading session. The warning signs are there all along the line. Northern Rock was a classic example. It did not go bust in one day.

Even when queues were forming in the streets outside the branches as desperate savers scrambled to get their hands on their own cash, the shares still had some value. Every day was a chance for shareholders, like savers, to salvage something from the wreckage before the shares eventually became worthless.

Case study: Cattles

Cattles is a sub-prime lender; in other words it lends to people who have difficulty in getting mortgages or bank loans.

Are alarm bells ringing?

They should have been the moment that the US sub-prime lending crisis started to unfold.

However, Cattles shares held up well throughout the early months of 2007 as the banking sector came under pressure and even applied to the Bank of England for a full banking licence.

Cattles came into the sub-prime crisis in good heart. Trading in 2006 had been slightly ahead of expectations with strong demand for the company's services producing double digit profit growth and keeping arrears and bad debts stable. The dividend was raised by 11.5%.

Indeed, in mid-year Cattles attempted to raise £400 in the bank syndication market and found that demand was so strong it ended up with £800 million. It also talked to London Scottish Bank about making an offer for its rival and, although this move fell through in February 2007, the problems were at London Scottish, not Cattles.

In March 2007 Cattles successfully placed 33 million shares at 403.25p, in line with the prevailing stock market price, to raise capital for expansion.

Growing concerns

However, it was around this time that concerns were growing over the banking system and although Cattles was still bullish about prospects it was natural to wonder how well its business model would stand up to the tightening credit system.

Although Cattles insisted at the end of 2007 that it was taking a conservative line on new loans, there were worrying signs. The loan book was expanding just as other lenders were clamping down. It was hard to see how Cattles could possibly be immune from the trends in the overall market.

(A similar phenomenon occurred at GEC, renamed Marconi, six years previously. While all other tech firms were belatedly admitting that sales were being lost and not merely postponed, Marconi continued to insist that all was well. Shareholders were eventually wiped out when the truth emerged.)

The markets did not believe the Cattles story and its shares slid steadily from a peak of 400p early in the year to 250p at the end.

Figure 15.1: Cattles

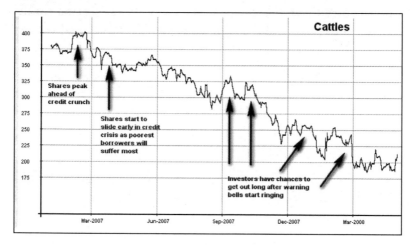

In April 2008 Cattles not only increased its banking facilities by £200 million but asked its shareholders to stump up a similar amount in a 9-for-20 rights issue priced at 128p, way below the then stock market price of around 200p. Despite claims of continuing strong trading, Cattles looked to be expanding at the wrong time.

One or two cracks in the edifice started to appear in the second half of 2008. Cattles began to tighten its lending criteria, turning more applications down, and it admitted that arrears had started to creep up.

On 11th December 2008 Cattles was forced by a downward movement in its share price to admit that its banking licence application was not going to plan. The FSA was proposing more stringent terms and the application was proceeding at a slower pace than expected.

Up to this point shareholders could be forgiven for keeping faith with Cattles despite the fall in its share price over the previous nine months.

- Trading had been described as strong and in line with expectations

- The dividend had increased

- Profits were growing quickly

- Arrears were under control.

Matters started to gather momentum, though, and later that same month Cattles headed its trading update with these ominous words:

> "Cattles has strong demand for its products. The Group is on course to deliver trading results in line with expectations in 2008 despite having deliberately reduced volumes in all businesses since February. Although affected by the current economic situation, our operating model is proving robust and arrears and impairment are within reasonable tolerances.

> "Despite this resilient trading performance, in the light of current market and economic conditions, we have decided it would be prudent not to propose a final dividend in respect of the year ending 31st December 2008, nor pay an interim dividend in respect of the six months ending 30th June 2009. This has the benefit of strengthening our capital ratios even further, thus aiding discussions with the FSA regarding our deposit taking licence application and with banks regarding wholesale funding. It also preserves cash within the business at a time when liquidity is vital."

Given that the credit crunch was really biting by now and the stock market was falling heavily, this surely was a time for Cattles shareholders to take the hint and sell. This last statement had the air of a management team trying hard not to face the reality of the changed situation, which is always a warning sign.

At this stage it was still possible to sell at around 250p, well below the 400p peak but considerably higher than the price available throughout 2006, and there had been some good dividends in the meantime.

Banking licence dropped

A month later Cattles withdrew its application for a banking licence as it became clear that it would not get one:

> "until the unprecedented turmoil in the financial markets has stabilised and the terms of the group's renegotiation of £635 million of its bank facilities are known."

Realistically it was never going to get a licence.

The following month results for 2008 were delayed 'pending completion of a review of the adequacy of its impairment provisions'.

In other words, it had not written off enough bad debt. Extra write-offs would push profits lower than the market was expecting. In fact, the write-offs totalled £700 million and covered previous years and the impact left Cattles in breach of its banking covenants.

At this point it was still not too late to get out at 200p, a remarkably high price given the scale of the debacle that was engulfing Cattles. Eventually the shares were worth only 1p.

It is admittedly easy to view the events with the benefit of hindsight. However, all the warning signs along the way should have alerted shareholders to the dangers of clinging on.

Tracking news announcements

Some shares you simply do have to keep an eye on. Certain sectors and individual companies tend to attract lots of news announcements and their shares may be volatile irrespective of the general economic trends.

In such cases you need to decide whether to grit your teeth for the long term or to move in and out as circumstances dictate. You should not, however, simply close your eyes and ignore what is going on. You can lose a lot of money if you refuse to face up to reality. Ask those who ignored the announcements from Northern Rock as the shares crashed and ultimately found themselves with worthless investments.

Case study: British Airways

The performance of British Airways shares offers important insights into managing risks.

At first glance this should be a solid company, a national institution with a global reach, big enough to survive tough trading conditions and with a widely recognised brand name.

Life has not been kind to BA over the years, however. Like its counterpart in the telecoms industry, BT, it has had to adapt to increasing competition and has not always been successful in doing so.

Competition has not only come from the flag carriers of rival nations. The growth of budget airlines has taken its toll to the extent that Ryanair actually overtook BA in terms of stock market capitalisation.

Like the banks, BA seems too big to be allowed to fail. It is the mainstay of the country's largest airport, Heathrow, occupying an entire terminal yet still spilling over into another terminal to mop up all its flights. BA is also a vital ingredient of Gatwick and the main Scottish airports.

Figure 15.2: BA

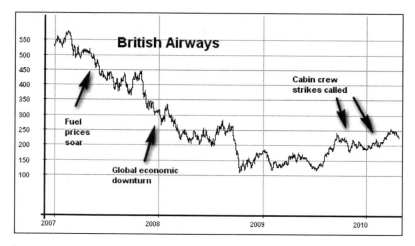

It would be wrong, however, to assume that the self-styled World's Favourite Airline is an investment you could lock away and forget about. Since the start of the millennium BA shares have fallen from 470p to 100p, zoomed to 550p (with a setback from 340p to 200p on the way) then tumbled again to little over 100p.

All this was driven by news announcements. You closed your eyes at your peril.

The whole airline industry has been driven by many factors: the price of fuel, foreign currency fluctuations, air passenger numbers, whether passengers are booking economy or first class, demand for air freight, whether short or long haul flights are in demand and the increase in competition are among the obvious ones.

No dividend

During the 2000s BA has seen turnover remain remarkably stable at around £8 billion yet the bottom line has fluctuated between a pre-tax profit of £908 million and a loss of £312 million. For most of the decade BA paid no dividend, the 5p allocated in 2009 being a rare beacon of hope before the airline plunged back into losses.

One reason for the non-payment of a dividend for so many years was the massive debt pile hanging like a millstone round BA. Cash generated from the operations reduced this drag from over £6 billion in 2002 to just under £1 billion in 2007 before net debts started to rise ominously again.

These figures, though, are part of the routine announcements that all companies make. To keep track of them you would need to check up on BA no more than twice a year at the time of half-yearly and annual results.

However, no one could accuse the airline industry of keeping the public in the dark. To keep abreast of your investment in BA you needed to watch out for monthly statements on traffic figures and how full the aircraft were, not only for BA but also for major rivals Easyjet and Ryanair.

Growth of competition

In a cut-throat market with budget rivals attempting to undercut BA on shorthaul routes it was important to keep watch on whether BA's strategy of boosting revenue on longhaul – luring business travellers rather than ordinary economy class passengers – was working.

To add to the spice, the number of carriers has over the years expanded and contracted as national carriers mushroomed, with emerging nations indulging in chauvinist flag waving, followed by governments agreeing to mergers rather than prop up loss-making macho enterprises.

Governments have also intervened through regulatory agencies. As airlines consolidated, objections arose to the potential loss of competition on certain routes. Near to home, the Irish government took fright when the upstart Ryanair launched a cheeky takeover bid for Aer Lingus, which would have meant only one carrier service for many Irish routes.

That's a lot going on and BA had the additional aggravation of the chaotic switch to Terminal Five at Heathrow and industrial action at different times by baggage handlers and cabin crew. In between all that it was negotiating a merger with Spanish airline Iberia.

How the news unfolded

This is the timetable of events in the early months of 2010. The bad news is in italics:

- **January 6**: *Reports passenger numbers down*, cargo up in December. Starts talks with cabin crew's union Unite in attempt to avert strike.

- **January 12**: Submission to US Department of Justice concerns over alliance with American Airlines, bargains with Japan Airline to stay in the alliance.

- **January 18**: *Starts training staff to replace cabin crews in event of strike.*

- **February 5**: Reports operating profit *but pre-tax loss* for third quarter to December 1.

- **February 12**: *Suspends 15 cabin crew over alleged intimidation.*

- **February 19**: Wins court case against cabin crew over changes to working practices.

- **March 3**: Traffic figures for February higher than in previous year.

- **March 5**: Negotiations with Unite continue.

- **March 12**: *Unite reveals strike plans after talks fail.*

- **March 17**: Concludes talks with unions on ending defined benefits pension scheme.

- **March 19**: *Talks with Unite to avert strike collapse.*

- **March 20**: *Three-day strike begins.*

- **March 22**: Profit outlook unchanged despite strike.

- **March 27**: *Four day strike of cabin crew begins.*

- **March 31**: *Fails to sign Iberia deal on time.*

- **April 7**: Talks resume with Unite.

- **April 8**: Merger agreement with Iberia signed.

- **April 15**: *Volcanic ash grounds all UK flights.*

Figure 15.3: BA

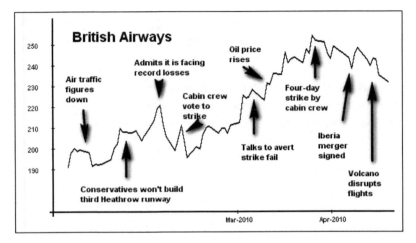

All these events had considerable implications for the British Airways share price and for whether investors saw this as a long term investment. We can see that good and bad news come in fairly equal instalments but we are surely looking for companies issuing more good news than bad. In difficult times, companies will always err on the side of putting the best gloss on the situation.

Also we should note that the bad news is quite serious and its potential effects far outweigh the promising factors. We know that a strike or series of strikes will have a serious impact that starts immediately and lasts long term. Passengers are encouraged to go elsewhere and, even if the union caves in, there will be a residue of ill feeling among staff.

The alliances with other airlines will help to boost passenger numbers in the future but putting together these alliances demands patient negotiations with other airlines and the regulators in various countries while the benefits are hard to quantify.

There were, therefore, plenty of warnings for investors to get out and to stay well clear. If a company announces a run of bad news, find one where the pronouncements are more favourable.

Now we really cannot blame BA for the prolonged shutdown of airports in the UK and Europe in April. However, investments are not built on sympathy.

What is surprising is not that BA shares fell back when the ash cloud burst on the scene. It is that the shares had fallen so little before then, leaving investors with the opportunity to cut their losses.

Case Study: BP

BP has been a highly volatile stock over the years, responding partly to how well the company was perceived as being run but more particularly to the price of crude oil, over which BP like other oil companies had little control.

Every $1 rise in crude flowed through to the profit line; likewise every reduction in the crude price was reflected pretty fully in a fall in profitability. This applied even though BP was a fully integrated oil company, that is it had operations at all levels including exploration, extraction, refining, distribution and retailing.

Its share price has reflected the vagaries of a market in which oil has risen from $40 a barrel to $160 before falling back to under $60 then recovering to around $80. Oil companies are committed to fixed costs such as for exploration or building refineries. When income falls it is difficult if not impossible to strip out a corresponding level of costs.

BP's share price has fluctuated considerably in response. It swung between 500p and 680p in the early part of the new millennium; then came a sharp fall to 350p in March 2003 followed by a steady rise to the top side of 700p exactly three years later; more fluctuations over 12 months preceded a heavy fall from 650p to 380p; then there was an erratic recovery to 650p in April 2010.

Figure 15.4: BP

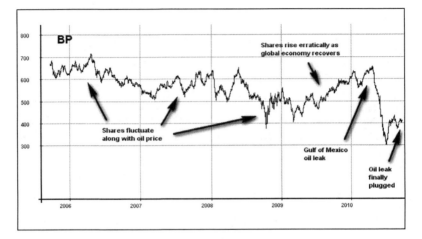

During that time annual turnover dropped from £110 billion to £95 billion, rose to £141 billion, peaked suddenly at £238 billion in 2008 when the oil price soared, then slumped to £148 billion. Profits were equally erratic.

However, the dividend remained steady throughout this period, dipping very slightly on two occasions but rising steadily in the majority of years. BP achieved this stability by varying the dividend cover between 1.25 times and three times.

At the peak of its share price, BP was offering a yield of 6.7%. It looked good.

There are various pointers to draw from all this. Firstly, long term investors could be perfectly happy to ride out the ups and downs of the oil price and BP's share price in the knowledge that the fluctuations would even themselves out and there would be a steadily improving dividend in the meantime. Secondly, those looking for short term gains could play the market, buying BP when the oil price rose and selling when it peaked.

Gulf of Mexico oil spill

Events took a nasty turn for the worse, though, on 20 April 2010 when the Deepwater Horizon drilling rig blew up in the Gulf of Mexico, killing 11 people and allowing several thousand barrels of oil a day to pour out.

No investor could reasonably have foreseen this, although it is true that BP's safety record had been criticised in the past, particularly in the wake of a previous disaster at Prudholme Bay in Alaska. Shareholders could not have known of what the US Senate subsequently referred to as a litany of disasters ahead of the catastrophic spill, including going ahead after the well failed pressure tests for potential gas leaks.

Nor was it readily obvious that this was the moment to get out of BP shares pronto. As long as the oil leak could be plugged quickly, BP would have had no more than a nasty setback.

However, the news worsened day by day. Attempts to plug the leak failed. It was a gargantuan task given that the broken pipe was 5000 feet below the ocean surface. Soon BP had 500 people working round the clock in Houston trying to contain the disaster.

Apart from stemming the flow, BP was attempting to contain the oil slick on the surface and prevent it from coming ashore. The company bought a third of the world's available supply of dispersants to break up the oil as rapidly as possible.

Costs mount

It became increasingly clear that the cost to BP would be substantial, even though there was some insurance cover. Apart from the cost of plugging the leak and cleaning up, which was escalating the longer it took to fix the seepage, there would inevitably be demands for compensation for the deaths and the devastation. The US authorities would impose fines for any breaches of safety regulations.

In addition, BP had lost revenue from the sale of the leaked oil. It was impossible to estimate the total cost but it was clear that BP's profits for the year would be severely dented and could be wiped out. Some estimates put the likely total costs, including lost revenue, at £15 billion.

There was a serious danger that BP would be unable to pay a dividend, or at least that the dividend would have to be reduced, despite assurances from BP that it was 'a big company with very big cash flows'.

BP had reported nearly £5 billion inward cash flow in the first quarter and had about £10 billion worth of undrawn borrowing facilities available. However, BP's capital spending is inevitably heavy. In 2009 capex plus the dividend exceeded free cash flow.

BP shares peaked at 655p on the day of the disaster, closing in London before the explosion. They fell comparatively slowly, not crossing below 600p until 10 calendar days and eight trading days after the disaster.

This was not a time for sentiment. There was no scope to sit back and tell yourself: 'BP has served me well in the past and it will all come out OK in due course.' The news was catalogued extensively in the press day by day.

It is vital not to assume that if you missed the best chance to get out it is too late to sell. Anyone acting a few days after the leak began would have got a better price than those who held on blindly as the shares slumped to 530p by the middle of May.

Indeed, optimists actually caused the BP share price to tick up several times during the fall, sometimes quite sharply, thus presenting slow moving shareholders with an opportunity to sell. Do not be fooled by these dead cat bounces. Speculative short selling would produce the occasional upward blip as those responsible took their profits by buying back at a lower level.

Presumably buyers were hoping that all the bad news was now allowed for in the lower share price but this was an enormous assumption to make. Why on earth take the risk when it was possible to switch into other oil companies such as Royal Dutch Shell, which did not have BP's horrendous problem?

It was wrong to be lured by a prospective yield of more than 7%, double the market average, and a P/E of 7.25 times compared with a market average of over 11 at that time. It was obvious that analysts would have to cut back their forecasts of BP's earnings and would probably have to trim estimates of the dividend, so these figures were effectively meaningless.

Timetable of events:

- **March 11**: BP pays £4.6 billion for US and South American assets of Devon Energy, giving vital foothold into Brazil's oil wealth. Shares peak.

- **April 21**: Oil rig explodes in Gulf of Mexico.

- **April 28**: Spillage worse than thought, President Obama says BP will pay full clean-up costs. Shares fall 7%.

- **May 2**: BP doubled amount spent daily on containing oil slick to nearly £4 million, estimates of extent of leak rise to 4.2 million gallons a day. Shares now down 13% since accident and they fall another 2% over the next two days.

- **May 24**: Preparations for fourth attempt to plug the leak. Shares fall 2.7%, now down 23% since accident.

- **May 25**: Possible failings in safety checks and equipment identified. Shares fall 2%.

- **June 1**: US attorney general begins criminal and civil investigation. Shares drop 13% after falling 17% at one point.

- **June 4**: Obama steps up pressure on BP to suspend dividends.

- **June 9**: Latest attempt to plug leak may have made matters worse. Dividend now in serious doubt. Shares fall 4%.

- **June 16:** BP suspends dividend to pay for £13.5 billion clean-up fund. Dividend due on June 21 will not be paid. Shares fall just 1.25p to 340.75p as decision is inevitable.

Taking some profits

Just as we may build our holding in a company in two or more tranches rather than at one go, we can choose to sell part rather than all of our holding in a company. We will occasionally see advice in newspapers to take some profits where a company's share price has risen strongly.

The idea is that you bank some profits as a safeguard against the shares dropping back but keep part of your holding so that you still gain if the shares continue to rise. It is a neat way of hedging our bets.

The strategy is particularly enticing where a share price has doubled since the purchase was made. We can sell half our stake to recoup all our initial outlay and keep the other half as a free play.

If this helps you to sleep more soundly at night, so be it, but it is a rather wishy-washy notion. Do we not have the courage of our convictions? Taking some profits means we can avoid taking a careful, rational decision on whether to stay in or get out.

Besides, what are we to do with the cash we raise from selling part of our holding? Unless we really needed it, we are going to invest it again, which means finding a better company.

Thus it makes sense to take profits only if we have somewhere better to park the cash, in which case we should surely be thinking of cashing in all our holding in that particular company rather than just part of it.

Lessons learnt

- Before you sell, ask yourself if you are going to do something better with the money you raise

- Be prepared to get out if there is good reason to fear that the share price will fall or the dividend will be reduced

- Be sure to read announcements from companies in your portfolio in case they contain bad news

- If you are forced to sell, keep a cool head and make a calm assessment of which shares should go

- Bear in mind the possibility of incurring capital gains tax.

Chapter 16.
Rights Issues and Placings

Right issues

If you invest in a range of companies over a period of time you are almost certainly going to find yourself on the receiving end of a rights issue at some point.

A rights issue is where you as an existing shareholder are offered the right to buy more shares at a specific price, usually at a lower level than the prevailing stock market price. These will be offered in a specific ratio to shares already held. For example, you may have the right to buy one new share for every three already held. Or the ratio may be more complex, such as 13 new shares for every 17 already held.

The ratio will depend on how much money the company needs to raise and how likely shareholders are to stump up. The more money the company needs, the more shares you will be offered in proportion to your existing holdings. In extreme cases you may be asked to buy more shares than you already hold.

At first sight a rights issue looks attractive. After all, you thought the company was worth investing in at some point in the past, and you have held onto the shares so far, so where is the great harm in adding to your holding? You have the bonus of getting the shares on the cheap instead of paying the full market price.

However:

- You cannot choose which company to invest in

- You will be told how many shares you are entitled to

- You will be given a limited period to decide whether to take up your entitlement.

There is worse. The share price of the company in question will almost certainly fall before you have the time to get out so you are rather stuck with the rights issue. It is true that sometimes you can foresee the possibility of a rights issue coming but this is frankly rare.

Warning signs include:

- Speculation in the press that a rights issue will be made

- A heavy debt burden that is holding the company back, especially if it has been borrowed on onerous terms such as a high interest rate

- A danger that the company will break its banking covenants, sparking expensive negotiations with the banks

- Rumours that the company is looking for acquisitions, especially if the company refuses to deny the rumours

- A danger that the company's credit rating could be revised downwards. These ratings affect the terms under which companies can borrow from banks or issue bonds. A higher rating improves the borrowing terms.

You may feel that, in a sense, the shares ought to be more attractive when a company proposes a rights issue. They now carry the right for the holder to get additional shares on the cheap.

Why the share price falls

However, rights issues are unpopular because investors expect companies to pay cash to the shareholders, not the other way round. The share price will fall on the stock market partly because some investors will dump their holdings rather than cough up more money.

They will also fall because the shares now really do have a different value. There will be more shares in issue so ownership of the company will be divided up among a greater number of shares and the share price will reflect this change in circumstances.

This is partly offset by the fact that the company will have a pile of cash that could be used to pay down debt, which will reduce the annual interest bill, or to fund expansion, which should improve profits.

The actual fall in the share price will reflect perceptions of how much better placed the company is to make increased profits in the future.

Nonetheless we must accept a double whammy: the value of our shares will fall and we face the prospect of stumping up more cash or losing out on the chance to buy cheaper shares.

On the whole, once a rights issue is announced, it makes more sense to hang on and take up our rights (assuming we can afford them). We then have a choice of:

- keeping all our newly augmented holding if we are happy that the company will put the cash it is raising to good use. In this way we are building our portfolio

- selling some shares after the rights issue has gone through if we have overstretched ourselves or if we are uncomfortable with a higher holding in the company

- selling the lot if we have lost confidence in the company's management to use the proceeds of the rights issue wisely, and look to build our portfolio elsewhere.

The folly of doing nothing

It is *not* a good idea to stick your head in the sand and ignore a rights issue. You will be sent a prospectus and you should at least read the main summary so you understand what is going on.

If you do nothing, then at best the company will sell your shares in the market. The company will take the rights issue price plus any expenses incurred and pay you any premium left over. You may not do as well out of the deal as you would have done taking up your entitlement because you will be selling at the same time as other shareholders who let their rights lapse.

In some rights issues you lose your entitlement if you do not buy the shares you are offered. In this case you have lost every advantage of the rights issue *and* seen a fall in the price of your existing holding.

Look in the prospectus and see what your options are. You will be asked how many new shares you wish to buy and how many new shares you wish to sell.

You do have the option of taking up your rights for some shares and selling the remaining rights to fund your purchase. This way you get some more shares without having to fork out, although you do not get your full entitlement. Be warned that trying to calculate how many shares to sell and how many to retain is extremely difficult and complicated because of possible changes in share prices between the announcement of the rights issue and the actual dishing out of the new shares. I have not found any formula that is simple and satisfactory.

In any case, if the rights issue is worth taking up you will surely want to grab your entitlement if you can afford it. Otherwise why not buy as many new shares as you can afford and opt to sell the rest?

Mix and match

You may be offered the opportunity of taking more or less than your entitlement. This option will be in the prospectus.

Companies may offer this facility because it greatly increases the chances of a full take up of the rights, since any rejected shares can be passed on to keener investors. This may remove the need to appoint underwriters.

Generally speaking, if as is usual the shares are being offered at a discount to the stock market price then it is advantageous to apply for extra shares as you are getting them on the cheap.

Nothing in stock market investing works all the time though. Barclays offered this facility in a rights issue to rescue its balance sheet during the credit crunch. It seemed very attractive at the time to apply for extra shares and most investors did so, which meant the extra allocation per investor was meagre.

That was perhaps as well: the financial crisis deepened and Barclays shares subsequently fell well below the rights issue price.

Case study: National Grid

Energy distribution company National Grid sprung a nasty shock on its shareholders in May 2010 when it proposed a rights issue to raise £3.2 billion. There was no chance to see this coming and to get out before the shares fell.

National Grid had repeatedly assured investors that it would not tap the equity markets for extra cash. Suddenly the company was saying that it needed to step up investment because the drive towards cleaner energy meant it had to make more connections to wind farms and other renewable energy sources and to make energy distribution more efficient.

This was all highly commendable but it was surely foreseeable for National Grid's executives that capital investment would need to be increased. The failure to communicate better with shareholders was a point against management.

This was one case where a threat to the company's credit rating, then standing at a respectable A (two notches down from the top rating of AAA), was a prime factor, as chief executive Steve Holliday admitted when he said in announcing the rights issue: 'We need to have the financial flexibility to maintain the credit ratings we have had over recent times.'

National Grid proposed capex spending of £22 billion over the following five years, so even with the proceeds of the rights issue and strong cash generation there would be a need for borrowing and hence a high credit rating. The company had already invested £14 billion over the previous five years.

Figure 16.1: National Grid

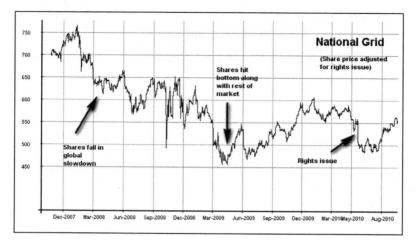

The energy company's shares fell 7%, from 620p to 576.5p, on the day of the rights issue announcement and a further 2% the following day. The fall would probably have been greater had the rights issue not accompanied strong annual results, which included an 8% rise in the dividend and a promise to keep increasing the dividend for another two years at least. Profits for the year that had just ended were up 12% to £2 billion despite a 10% fall in revenue to £14 billion.

The proposed rights issue was for investors to subscribe for two new shares for every five held. This was quite a chunky slab so the rights price was set at 335p, a 44% discount on the previous closing level of 620p, to tempt investors to take up their entitlement.

On balance, it was right to hold on and subscribe to the rights issue for the following reasons:

- The deep discount meant that taking up rights made financial sense for the investor as the new shares would be worth substantially more than the purchase price.

- Major institutional investors said they would take up the rights, guaranteeing that the issue would be a success and removing the need for expensive underwriting.

- The strong results indicated that management was on the right track and could be forgiven the solecism of the shock announcement.

- The promise of a rising dividend made holding the shares more attractive for the many shareholders who had bought for income in the first place.

Grandiose schemes

Beware the grandiose scheme. People who set out to conquer the world are likely to find themselves lying dead on the battlefield. The deal of the century may well be remembered as a disaster rather than a masterstroke.

We noted in an earlier chapter that small, digestible deals can be an excellent way to grow the company. Large deals are liable to wreck it.

The bigger the bid, the greater the challenge to make it work. Shareholders should consider whether any large deal has more to do with the ego of the chief executive than the future success of the enlarged company.

Two banks – RBS in the acquisition of ABN Amro and Lloyds TSB in the takeover of HBoS – found that the deal of the century turned into a bailout by the government.

In such cases it is right to bite the bullet and get out after a rights issue is announced, albeit at a lower price than we would have got with the benefits of clairvoyance. Taking this course of action will inevitably be easier if we are at least banking a profit on our original investment but the decision should be made on the basis of whether we have lost confidence in management and the company, not on what has happened previously.

Case study: Prudential

Tidjane Thiam had been installed as chief executive of insurance giant Prudential for only a matter of months before he unveiled one of the most audacious bids of all time: the $35.5 billion (£23 billion at the then exchange rate) offer for the Asian assets of struggling American rival AIG.

There was, it had to be said, much to commend this move in principle. Prudential's performance before Thiam's arrival had been somewhat pedestrian. His plan was to move into the fast growing Asian market, creating one of the world's largest insurance groups in the process.

Furthermore, AIG needed to strike a deal. It had been one of the highest profile bailouts in the American financial crash.

Prudential called it 'a compelling chance' to create South East Asia's leading insurer. Such ambitions are fine provided you have the money to pay for them but Pru did not. It proposed to raise $21 billion (£14 billion), more than half the purchase price, through the largest rights issue the UK had ever seen.

Institutional investors naturally questioned whether the Pru was getting such a good deal before they were prepared to stump up the cash. After all, the UK had not yet recovered from its own financial collapse and the flow of cash in the economy was still sluggish.

Figure 16.2: Prudential

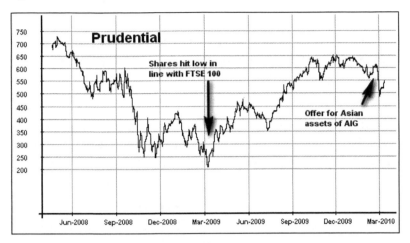

Shares in Prudential immediately fell 12% after the proposed deal was announced in February 2010, closing down 72p at 530p after hitting 515p at one point.

It was not too late for nervous private investors to get out, though. Prudential's share price had more than tripled since plumbing a low of 200p in March 2009 so a correction was probably overdue anyway.

After dipping below 500p at the beginning of March the shares clawed back up to 580p, surely quite high enough given the cash call hanging over shareholders. Besides, serious concerns were raised over the high price that the Pru was paying for the assets. Given the financially stricken state of AIG, it did not look as if Thiam had driven a particularly hard bargain.

The company was adamant that it would not be knocked off course. Chairman Harvey McGrath proclaimed:

> "We are entirely committed to the transaction. The work completed since 1 March with the AIA and Prudential teams has convinced me more than ever that the enlarged group will be in a position to capture sustainable and highly profitable

growth and will deliver substantial long term value for our shareholders."

Do not be swayed by such words. That is the sort of thing that they always say. You needed to judge the merits of the deal for yourself.

Rights issue terms

Shareholders were asked to buy 11 new shares for every two already held. To get such a large number of extra shares away, they were offered at a bargain basement 104p each.

Serious concerns were immediately raised as to whether Prudential was overpaying for these admittedly attractive assets. It was also fair to question whether this deal was simply too big for Prudential. The £14.5 billion rights issue was as large as Prudential's existing stock market capitalisation. In effect, shareholders were being asked to double their stakes.

Even then, the rights issue was not enough to fund the whole purchase, so Thiam was faced with borrowing heavily and selling some assets to bridge the gap.

There were worrying wobbles along the way. Details of the rights issue were delayed for nearly two weeks as Pru sought to reassure the Financial Services Authority that it had sufficient capital.

Then there was controversy over the underwriting terms on the rights issue. Institutions were offered fees of 2% for agreeing to take any shares rejected by shareholders, compared with 1.75% in other recent rights issues at the time.

Prudential was, in fact, paying a total of £1.35 billion in fees to advisers on the deal, a great boost to the struggling finance system but effectively money that was being siphoned off in addition to the price of the deal itself.

In the event the deal fell through after Prudential attempted to negotiate a reduction in the agreed price for AIA, leaving Thiam and McGrath sitting very uncomfortably with their strategy in ruins.

Rights issues at or near the market price

Just occasionally a rights issue is made at or near the prevailing stock market price. Possibly the company has been doing particularly well and institutional investors are clamouring for larger stakes in the success story.

In such cases you will not lose out if you fail to take up your entitlement as you are not passing up the chance to acquire shares on the cheap. However, you will probably be happy to buy more shares in a successful company, provided you have the ready cash.

Placings and open offers

As an alternative to a rights issue, a company may choose to place shares with institutional investors as a way of raising money. The advantages are:

- It is cheaper to place shares with a few investors rather than communicate with the whole share register

- It is more certain than a rights issue because the company can sound out institutions beforehand to see how many shares they are willing to take and at what price

- The pricing of the issue can be set at the highest possible level because the company knows what the market will stand

- There is no need to pay underwriting fees.

You do not have to do anything in the case of a placing, except possibly vote to approve it at an EGM if the board has not previously been given permission by shareholders to place sufficient shares.

A placing may be accompanied by an open offer to existing shareholders giving them the right to subscribe for some of the new shares at the same price as the placing.

This can be a comparatively easy decision to make. The placing price is likely to be only just below the current stock market price so you are less likely to feel you are missing out if you fail to take up your allocation.

Special dividends and share buybacks

In contrast to issuing new shares, companies may decide to buy their own existing shares and cancel them. Share buybacks come in and out of fashion and there is disagreement over whether they do any good. Fortunately investors do not have to take any action or make any difficult decisions.

The issuing of new shares dilutes existing holdings; if you have invested in a company that buys back shares then your holding rises fractionally as a percentage of the total, since there will be fewer shares in existence while your holding stays the same.

As a general rule companies propose buybacks when they are generating more cash than they know what to do with. Cash can be used to fund the growth of the business, buy other businesses or reduce cash. If none of these options seems attractive to the board of directors they can either build a massive cash pile or hand the money to the shareholders.

It may be difficult for a company with a dominant position to acquire other companies in the same sector without provoking the ire of the competition authorities; on the other hand it can be dangerous to try to diversify into new businesses that the directors do not fully understand.

Handing over the loot can take two forms: a one-off special dividend or a share buyback.

Advantages of a special dividend are that all shareholders benefit equally. Disadvantages are that shareholders may be landed with a sizeable tax bill on the dividends and the pattern of payouts will be distorted because the special dividend is unlikely to be repeated the following year.

The advantage of a share buyback is that it tends to prop up the share price by mopping up sellers. In theory dividends should improve in future as profits will be divided among fewer shares.

The disadvantage is that if you do not want to sell there is no immediate gain for you.

Critics of share buybacks argue that:

- this is not really returning cash to shareholders in the way that dividends do

- buybacks imply that the board is bereft of ideas to grow the business

- buybacks rarely prompt a rise in the share price, which often drifts lower despite the support from the company

- increasing the dividend is more likely to drive the share price higher than buybacks

- reducing debt is more beneficial than buying back shares. Borrowing to fund buybacks, as sometimes happens, is storing up potential trouble for the future if the cash flow dries up

- a buyback is equivalent to a rights issue in that those shareholders who do not sell all or part of their holdings end up with what is effectively a larger percentage of the company.

A fair alternative is for companies to buy back a proportion of shares from all shareholders. In that way everyone benefits equally. However, this is more bitty and expensive than buying shares in the market so companies rarely pursue this option.

BP spent £23 billion on share buybacks over several years since the millennium. Shareholders would have been better off with increased dividends while the good times rolled. Similarly mining group Anglo American went on a buyback spree and subsequently found itself suspending its dividend in 2010.

These are admittedly extreme cases. Usually buybacks leave the dividend to be divided among fewer shares so if you are investing for income you can usually just sit tight if a company you invest in starts a share buyback programme. Just be aware of the possible dangers.

Lessons learnt

- Rights issues tend to be unpopular because you are asked to put up money that you would otherwise not have invested in that company at that stage

- Consider your options carefully

- It is usually best to take up your rights of you can afford to and, if you wish, you can sell some shares in the market after the issue has gone through

- With placings you may have the right to buy some shares. The price is unlikely to be as attractive as in a rights issue and there is therefore less pressure on you to take up your entitlement.

Chapter 17.
Takeovers and Demergers

Takeovers

When you own shares in a company that is the target of a takeover bid there are clear, immediate advantages. With very rare exceptions, you will be offered more for your holding than you could have sold it for on the stock exchange. You cash in your profit (or at least cut your loss) within a few weeks at the most and move on to your next investment.

When you hold shares in the bidder, the advantages are less obvious and usually less immediate. Your shares are likely to fall in value, at least in the short term, as the market worries over whether the bidder is overpaying.

In general terms, any benefits from making takeovers tend to come later as the target company is integrated and cost savings are achieved. There may also be genuine synergies, where more products can be sold to the combined clientele.

It will all take time to settle down, though, and redundancy payments to persuade surplus staff to depart have to be paid now while the reduced wage bill shows through in the following year's results.

Cost savings are often dressed up as synergies but they are not the same: synergies grow the combined business, cost cutting shrinks it. The bidder all too often ends up damaging the assets that it was so keen to acquire.

A takeover bid for a company you own shares in is normally a pleasant experience. Bids are usually pitched at a higher level than the prevailing stock market price, so you see an instant uplift even where a bid is still only a twinkle is another company's eye.

There are in this instance many more imponderables to consider:

- How likely is a bid if one has not yet been made?

- Will there be more than one bidder?

- Can the bidder be persuaded to raise his offer?

- How likely is the bidder to walk away?

On the whole, it is better to hold on to the bitter end in a bid situation since the downside is limited. If the worst comes to the worst, the shares are unlikely to fall back below their previous level, so all that has happened is that we have lost the opportunity for a quick gain.

Once a company is seen to be potentially vulnerable to a takeover, the share price may hold up on hopes that another bidder will emerge or the original bidder will return with an offer high enough to secure the approval of the target company's board.

The potential upside is that a bid battle occurs and the price is pushed substantially higher.

A takeover situation is one phenomenon where you need to micromanage your investment. You need to check for developments every day and, if necessary, adjust your decision on whether to sell out or hold on in the light of the latest developments.

Bids are naturally of greater interest for those seeking capital gains rather than income. If the company is paying regular, well covered dividends then the case for holding on is greater. If the bid fails, you still get the dividends that you wanted in the first place.

Do not accept in haste ...

It is best not to act hastily if a company in which you own shares is the subject of a takeover offer. The worst outcome is that the suitor walks away and the company carries on as before; the best scenario is that you pocket a large capital gain accompanied by a dividend.

Accepting immediately will tie up your shares, depriving you of the opportunity to accept a better rival bid or to sell in the market.

In particular you should ignore the exhortations of the rival sides in a hostile takeover urging you to take precipitate action. Bids rarely go through on the first nod and if you miss the first deadline for acceptances there will almost always be a second and a third. If the bid fails at the first hurdle, your comparatively small holding would hardly have saved the day.

That is not the same as ignoring the situation. You should read the documents sent to you and, if these seem complicated to you, follow the developments in the press.

... until the outcome is certain

If it becomes clear that a takeover is certain to succeed, for instance if the bidder gains control of 51% of the shares, then accept without delay even if you are bitterly opposed to the offer. The sooner you accept, the sooner you get your cash. You do not want to be trapped in a company as a minority shareholder at the mercy of a controlling interest.

When a bidder gains control of more than 90% of the target company's shares it can force the last recalcitrant shareholders to accept anyway. They do not get more money, they just wait longer for their dosh.

What to do with the proceeds?

If a company in your portfolio is taken over you will obviously need to consider a replacement. Assuming your aim is a balanced portfolio, your first port of call should naturally be the same sector – assuming that there is another attractive stock there.

When the sector is consolidating, this may be difficult. Expectations of further bids may have forced shares in other possible targets to a higher price than you are willing to pay.

You do not have to replace like with like: there may be nothing similar that appeals. Do not go into the same sector just for the sake of it if you feel that there are better opportunities elsewhere.

Nonetheless, if you felt that the sector was worth one investment the same attractions that brought you to your original stock may apply to rivals. There is the added bonus that, if the sector is seeing consolidation, you may pick another takeover candidate.

Remember that other investors in the same situation as yourself will be thinking along similar lines. If you fancy another stock in the sector but baulk at its recently increased share price, it may be worth holding off to see if the share price settles back on profit taking.

Alternatively, you could try to get in first. By selling in the market as soon as a takeover is announced you can make the switch before the slow movers. You will probably not get the full takeover price by selling in the market – the market price will allow a discount to compensate for the time lag before the takeover goes through and for the risk that the bid may collapse – but you do get your cash faster.

Bear in mind that if you sell straight away you miss out if a rival bid is launched at a higher level so take a rational judgement on whether an alternative bid is a reasonable proposition. You will note that, if the market price rises above the existing offer, investors are assuming that a higher bid will appear from somewhere.

Case study: Forth Ports

Forth Ports shares jumped more than 25% on March 6th, 2010, after the company rejected a £612 million takeover approach from a group of existing major investors, including Arcus European Infrastructure Fund which held 23.5% of Forth, and Peel Ports with 3.5%.

In fact, there had been two approaches from the same source, the first at 1285p and the second at 1340p. Forth shares rose 286p to 1403p as the market took the view that it would need a bid of 1500p to succeed.

Figure 17.1: Forth

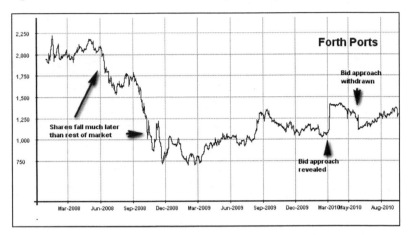

Arcus was formed in a management buyout of Babcock & Brown's European infrastructure business, which included the stake in Forth. This stake had been bought at close to 2000p two years earlier. Because of the time lag, Arcus was not obliged to offer a similar price to other shareholders.

Forth Ports operated seven UK ports including Tilbury and Grangemouth but, more importantly, it also owned more than 1000 acres of land in Scotland, most of it prime land on the Edinburgh waterfront. Some land previously owned by Forth had already been developed under lucrative arrangements.

There were several arguments in favour of Forth Ports shareholders hanging on rather than taking quick profits.

Firstly, Forth was the last major UK ports company still up for grabs. Associated British Ports, owner of 21 commercial and passenger ports, was bought by a consortium led by Goldman Sachs in 2006.

P&O, with its container terminal at Tilbury, was snapped up by Dubai World the same year.

Peel Ports had already bought Clydeport and Mersey Docks & Harbour Company. So this was the last chance for any other predator seeking a foothold in UK ports. In fact, UK utilities generally, including electricity suppliers and water companies, had been sought out by foreign buyers. Attractive UK assets were in short supply so there was a real possibility that the approach to Forth would flush out other interested parties.

Secondly, although there was no reason that would force Arcus to pay over the odds, there was a distinct chance of another predator recognising the value of the Forth property portfolio and starting a bidding war.

Forth rejected the Arcus approach as 'opportunistic', the meaningless tag traditionally given to all rejected bids. Forth's plans to develop its properties had shrunk along with the property market but there would inevitably be a rebound as markets recovered.

It planned to apply for planning consent for a £1.7 billion development of biomass plants in four Scottish ports to generate 500 megawatts of electricity in partnership with Scottish & Southern Energy.

In the event the bid was dropped on 27th May 2010 and the shares settled just below 1200p. While shareholders had lost the opportunity of getting a higher price for their shares they could feel that prospects were encouraging and it was possible that a bid could be agreed at a later date. Meanwhile dividends were being paid so it was right to hold on to see what developed.

Case study: VT

Defence group VT found itself in the unusual position of fighting two takeover battles at the same time in the early months of 2010.

VT was attempting to diversify by offering the equivalent of £330m for maintenance group Mouchel. This takeover was to be paid for in VT shares, so although VT would not be straining its cash resources it would be diluting the holdings of existing shareholders.

On 16th February Babcock, which maintains Britain's submarine fleet, made a £1.1 billion approach for VT, which was rebuffed as 'strategically unsound' and 'totally unacceptable'.

Well, it made a change from 'opportunistic' but the phraseology was meaningless. In fact the combining of the defence interests of VT and Babcock did make strategic sense, which is why Babcock came forward in the first place.

Figure 17.2: VT

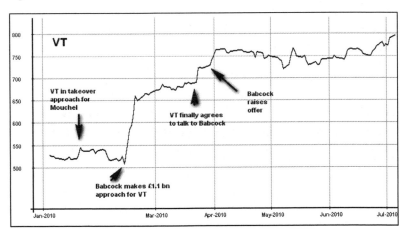

A more accurate reflection of the situation was that VT shares rose by 15% on the approach while Mouchel dropped by 12%. Better to hold shares in a target company than a bidder. VT had already raised its offer for Mouchel and there were fears that it would overpay if it persisted.

VT's argument was that it had spent five years getting out of shipbuilding, culminating in the sale of its stake in a shipbuilding and repairing joint venture to partner BAE Systems, and therefore a link with Babcock made no sense.

However, that would be Babcock's problem, not VT's.

As is so often the case when a bid is rebuffed, Babcock came back with a higher offer, just as VT had done for Mouchel, pushing VT's share price higher. In these circumstances the strength of the target company's board is vital. However inevitable capitulation seems, a strong defence will extract more goodies for the shareholders.

First, VT held back from opening its books to Babcock for as long as possible despite pressure from large shareholders in both companies. This kept Babcock guessing. It also hinted at making a bumper cash payout to shareholders and kept open the possibility of agreeing to a higher bid.

In early March advisers to the two sides held talks and eventually Babcock was persuaded to come up with a cash and shares combination that valued VT at 754p a share compared with Babcock's original offer of 634p.

There is always a danger, as happened at Forth, that the target company's board will overplay their hand and drive the bidder away. In this case a skillful defence extracted the maximum benefit for shareholders. It is better to put up a fight than to cave in meekly.

Shareholders who held on were richly rewarded. The final offer represented a 48% premium to VT's share price before Babcock declared its interest in making a bid.

Demergers

You may feel with so many companies keen to make acquisitions that bigger is more beautiful. Yet you are more likely to get added value from a company that splits up than from one that embarks on a takeover spree.

Chief executives generally prefer to preside over growing empires, human nature being what it is. However, you may occasionally find yourself holding shares in a company that proposes a demerger – that is, it either breaks into two or more pieces or it hives off part of the business that can stand alone.

When this happens, you will probably read of a 'sum of the parts' valuation. Analysts calculate what they think parts of the business would be worth as separate entities, either in stock market capitalisation or if sold to an interested buyer.

Add the parts together and if the total comes to more than the current stock market valuation of the group then it is to the benefit of shareholders to split up.

Among companies that have split one way or another are magazine publisher and exhibitions organiser EMAP, oil company Petrofac, property group Liberty International and telecoms group Carphone Warehouse.

It is hard to pinpoint quite when and where companies are prompted to decide to demerge. It does tend to follow a bout of cost cutting, with simplifying the business seen as the next logical step.

Demergers tend to happen in rising markets. No chief executive wants the ignominy of extolling the virtues of a split as enhancing shareholder value only to see the aggregate share prices drop below the previous level for the combined group.

Benefits of demergers

UBS analyst Daniel Stillit studied 75 European spin-offs completed between 2000 and 2009 and found that they had outperformed the stock market by an average of 16% over the following year.

He found that two out of three companies spun off from a larger group were bought or merged with another company at a premium.

The lesson is that, if you have invested in a company that proposes a demerger, it is generally good practice to hold on, vote for the demerger and retain any shareholdings you end up with to see what develops.

Case Study: Cable & Wireless

The first indication that international telecommunications group Cable & Wireless was considering splitting into two separate companies, each with a stock exchange listing, came in July 2007 but it was to be a further two and three quarter years before it all came to pass.

In the meantime, the shares followed an erratic but generally downward path as the C&W board appeared to be distracted by other considerations.

C&W was a relic of the colonial age that had successfully reinvented itself as a player on the UK stage as well as retaining extensive operations in the Caribbean, two businesses that did not fit particularly well together.

While the telecoms arm of the General Post Office, subsequently spun off as British Telecoms, ran the government monopoly on UK residential and business phones at home after the second world war, Cable & Wireless tended to the needs of the far flung but soon shrinking British Empire.

C&W always claimed that it exercised commendable self restraint in charges imposed on the countries where it operated; critics claimed it exploited its monopoly position. Whatever the rights and wrongs of the situation, emerging Commonwealth countries wanted to run their own communications systems. By the 1970s, C&W was taking more than half its revenue and profits from Hong Kong.

When Hong Kong was spun off, that effectively left a handful of Caribbean nations still relying on the British international carrier. Then BT lost its UK monopoly and C&W took the opportunity to develop a UK business.

That short history lesson explains how C&W executive chairman Richard Lapthorne came to be announcing a parting of the ways for the two discrete parts of the group. At the 2007 AGM, Lapthorne explained that finance director Tony Rise had told major investors that the group would 'look at the possibility of a demerger' to take place some time the following year.

Already C&W had been operating for a year as two standalone businesses, one based on the Europe, Asia and US operations (mainly the UK side) and the international operations covering Panama, Macau, Monaco and the Channel Islands lumped in with the Caribbean.

Lapthorne had been considering standing down as chairman but he told the AGM that his tenure had been extended to smooth the path to demerger. He argued that fixing a date for his departure would set an 'arbitrary timetable' for completing the demerger.

Perhaps a deadline would have concentrated a few minds, for ten months later little progress seemed to have been made. Presenting strong annual results and a positive outlook, Lapthorne could go no further than to confirm that demerger plans were being reviewed.

Figure 17.3: Cable & Wireless

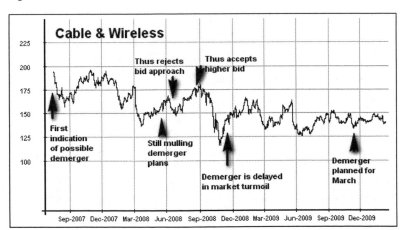

So, too, were other possible 'options for value realisation' such as selling some assets or borrowing against assets and handing the cash to shareholders. It was beginning to look like indecisiveness, especially when Rice said management was still collecting data and a decision would be made within the current financial year, which had another ten months to run.

Perhaps management was getting distracted, for just a month later C&W made a takeover approach for smaller rival Thus. The approach was rejected and C&W concentrated over the next two months on putting together a better offer and winning over the Thus board.

Another distracting issue was a hole in the pension fund which had to be plugged before a demerger was practicable.

Valuable time had been lost while the global economic crisis developed and soon C&W has forced to abandon its demerger plans, citing 'market turmoil' as the reason.

The argument for demerging what were effectively two separate businesses eventually resurfaced in November 2009. Cable & Wireless Worldwide emerged as a spin-off from Cable & Wireless Communications four months later.

Lessons learnt

- Do not rush to accept a takeover offer – there is plenty of time to make up your mind

- Do not be bullied into a decision by either side in a hostile takeover

- It is generally best to hang on to the end in a takeover situation rather than sell in the market

- Monitor the situation carefully and take the decision that you feel is right for you.

Chapter 18.
Costs and Taxes

Costs

There are inevitably costs involved with building a share portfolio. The London Stock Exchange's running costs have to be financed and the stock brokers who execute the deals on your behalf also want their cut.

If you want advice from your broker, that is an extra cost. So too are the salaries of analysts who research listed companies and issue insights into possible investments.

Ultimately, these costs have to be borne, directly or indirectly, by the investors who benefit from the services.

Fortunately these costs are, on the whole, quite reasonable but they should be borne in mind. The more services you get, the more you have to pay for and this cost has to be recouped, either in the form of dividends or from rising share prices, before you start to register a profit.

Before you start investing, check with your broker what type of service you are being offered and what the costs are. You may be offered:

- **Execution only**
  You decide which companies you wish to invest in and how many shares to buy. The broker does nothing for you other than carry out the trade as you specify. Not all brokers offer this service as it is the least lucrative from their point of view. Online brokers may offer nothing else.

- **Advisory service**

  You will be sent analysts' reports on companies covered by the broker and you may be phoned up with hot tips. Fees for this service vary. You still decide what companies you want to buy shares in and the size of each investment.

- **Discretionary service**

  The broker takes control and makes investments for you based on the amount you have available and your investment objectives such as attitude to risk. This is the most expensive option and you are relying on the broker to perform much better than you would yourself.

I would hope that after you have read this book you will feel able to run your own portfolio.

Stock broker charges

The cheapest way to invest is to set up an online account. You will pay typically £10 per trade for buying and selling, although some online brokers charge £12.50 or even £15. There may be an annual fee of up to £35, although most online brokers do not make this charge. Some brokers offer reduced fees going as low as £6 a trade if you make a minimum number of trades, say 15 or 25 a month. Do not make excessive numbers of trades just to fulfil a quota. Unless you are an active trader seeking short term profits, assume you are paying the full whack.

The Money.co.uk web site has a useful table comparing online stockbrokers (**www.money.co.uk/share-dealing.htm**) – although, as with all market comparison websites, the list is not exhaustive.

If you deal by telephone there will probably be a minimum charge of about £25. Commission may vary according to the size of the deal, with say 1.75% on deals worth up to £15,000 and 0.85% for larger deals. This percentage charge for larger deals is lower because the cost to the stock broker of carrying out your trade is virtually unchanged whatever the size of the deal.

On the basis of the charge quoted, a trade worth £1400 would cost £25; for £14,000 the cost is £245; for £140,000 it would be £1190.

These figures are for illustration only and will vary from broker to broker. Do not hesitate to ask what the charges are, or look under frequently asked questions on the broker's website.

The spread

At any given time there will be a gap between the buying and selling prices for stocks. This is known as the spread. For example, as I write this sentence I see that the bid-offer price for Tesco is 430.00 – 430.15, meaning that you can buy Tesco shares at 430.15p or sell them at 430.00p.

For actively traded shares the spread is set electronically, as brokers and professionals with access to the London Stock Exchange trading system post the prices at which they seek to buy or sell shares. The spread is the difference between the lowest price that any seller of the share is willing to accept and the highest price any prospective buyer is willing to pay.

For larger companies the spread is unlikely to be more than 1p and can be as low as 0.15p.

Smaller less actively traded companies may have the spread set by market makers – stock brokers that guarantee under LSE rules to buy and sell shares in specific companies. In these cases spreads are quite likely to be 2p and will be greater at times of share price volatility. The less well traded the shares, the wider the spread is likely to be.

Technically you are showing a loss on paper as soon as you buy any shares, a loss equivalent to the spread. That initial loss can be quite considerable if you buy penny shares.

For instance, currently I see that software developer ViaLogy has a buying price of 3.5p and a selling price of 3p. Although the spread is only 0.5p, the selling price was 14% lower than the buying price. If you bought £1000 worth of these shares and sold immediately, you would have lost about £170 after allowing for dealing costs and stamp duty.

You would need the selling price to rise by 33% to 4p to make the transaction profitable.

Such considerations are extremely important if you are an active trader hoping to turn a profit within days or even hours. They are much less of a worry for long term investors. After all, you do not suffer a loss – or make a profit – until you actually sell. Share prices will move over time and the spread will be wiped out by any gain in the share price or any dividend received.

Taxes

There are four taxes that can affect stock market investors:

- **Stamp duty**
  Charged at 0.5% of the value of all share purchases but not on share sales. You have to pay this tax whether you make a profit or not and it does reduce the size of your investment, albeit by only half a percent.

- **Income tax**
  Dividends received are added to your income and you pay tax at your top rate.

- **Capital gains tax**
  Charged on the difference between what you sell shares for and what you paid for them in the first place. The 2010 emergency Budget after the general election retained the £10,100 annual tax free allowance and set the rate of tax at 18% for basic rate taxpayers and 28% for higher rate taxpayers. Note that any gain above the allowance is added onto your income so it could take you into a higher tax bracket.

- **Inheritance tax**
  The value of any shares that you hold when you die will be added
  to your estate. Most shares quoted on AIM are exempt after they
  have been held for two years – exceptions are land and property,
  finance, legal and accountancy services, farming and forestry, and
  managing hotels or nursery homes.

While it is illegal to evade tax it is perfectly legitimate to structure
your portfolio to minimise your liability to pay tax. The most obvious
way is to use up your ISA (Individual Savings Account) allowance
each year. In 2010 the allowance stood at £10,200.

ISAs

The tax concession has existed in various forms since Prime Minister
Margaret Thatcher set out to create a home owning, share investing
society. Such investments have been called Tessas and PEPs. Now
they masquerade as Individual Savings Accounts.

The basic principle remains the same. Up to a specific limit set in the
Chancellor of the Exchequer's annual Budget, investors are rewarded
with tax exemptions to encourage them to claim their share of the
riches of the City of London.

AIM shares cannot be put into ISAs. The rationale for this slightly
bizarre state of affairs is that AIM shares are treated as unquoted,
although they patently are quoted on a recognised stock exchange.

ISAs have two tax advantages, one for all investors and one for higher
rate tax payers:

- **Capital gains**
  All shares held in an ISA are free of capital gains and you do not
  have to declare any gain to the taxman when you sell your shares.
  Since you are likely to hold shares long term in an ISA the chances
  of a considerable capital gain make this a very worthwhile
  advantage.

- **Income**

  Dividends from shares are paid net of tax irrespective of whether they are in an ISA. If you are a basic rate tax payer or do not pay income tax at all it makes no odds to you whether your shares are in an ISA or not. However, higher rate tax payers do not have to declare dividends paid into an ISA and therefore do not have to pay the higher rate tax on these earnings. If the shares are held outside an ISA they must be declared and extra tax will be charged.

Hares are not the only creatures to go mad in March. Investors who realise that their ISA entitlements for the financial year to 5th April are about to expire rush to make investments before it is too late.

Tax issues are secondary

The question is: should we invest simply to wring tax concessions from the grasping Chancellor? On the whole, avoiding tax should be a secondary consideration to sound investment decisions.

Let us take the AIM issue first. It is natural to want to do one's best for one's children (though the inheritance tax concession is pretty useless to you if you do not have any or if your estate is below the tax threshold).

However, you would surely be happy to see your investment double in price, leaving your children to pay 40% tax on the enlarged assets and still pocket some profit, rather than buy tax-free shares and see them fall in value.

In other words, it is the quality of the investment that matters. Poorly performing shares, bought just because they can be passed on tax-free, are a meagre inheritance. And while you live, you will be receiving dividends from a strong performer against possibly nothing from a weak company.

The lesson: do not cut your nose off to spite your face.

Certainly, if you see an investment you want to make anyway and it turns out to be free of any tax burden, then that is a bonus. But the investment side of the equation comes first. Remember that AIM is more lightly regulated and the criteria for joining less onerous than for the main market. The chances of an AIM company going bust or never paying a dividend are correspondingly greater.

Benefits of ISAs

ISAs do, on the other hand, have real benefits and they are for you and not your heirs. Legally avoiding income tax is worthwhile for higher rate taxpayers; the capital gains benefit is less clear cut.

The income tax allowance is available every year while a shares sale is a one-off event. Once you have sold shares that formed part of an ISA you cannot put other shares in their place. The allowance is lost for ever.

However, if you hold shares for the long term you could well run up a sizeable capital gain on your holdings over the years, so when you do come to sell you could avoid quite a hefty tax bill.

If you are investing in shares traded on the London Stock Exchange's main board you may as well put them into an ISA up to your allowance. You have nothing to lose and you may gain.

Even if you are an active trader but also like to keep some shares for the longer term, it is obviously sensible to put the long term investments into your ISA account and enjoy the benefits for all eternity.

Distortions of tax concessions

The problem with tax concessions is that they distort the market and they distort investment decisions. Thus you are encouraged to use up your full entitlement each year and to hang onto the shares.

If you feel that shares will fall or companies will be forced to scrap their dividends to conserve cash in hard times, what is the point of investing just to use up your tax exemption entitlement? If you lose money you will not have to pay tax anyway.

So think this through sensibly. Try to spread your ISA investments over the full financial year so you do not find yourself scrabbling round at the last minute for something to fill up your reservoir.

Are you going to get long term benefits from your ISA shares or are you investing just for the sake of it? If you have held off from investing for 11 months of the financial year because you are worried about the state of the economy or the state of the stock market, why plunge in with hasty decisions in the 12th month?

One crumb of comfort if you do end up paying tax on your investments is that, aggravating as it is to pay tax, you can console yourself with the thought that you are paying tax only because you made profits.

Offsetting capital gains

There is one situation where it is worth making a decision based on a tax advantage.

Supposing you are about to incur a capital gain on the sale of a stock that is not in your ISA and the amount exceeds your tax allowance for the year.

You should first consider whether it is possible to spread the sale over two tax years and thus halve the capital gain in each. This may not be possible. You may be selling because you need the cash or the company is being taken over. In such cases timing may be out of your control.

Alternatively you may feel that the shares in question are about to fall and that time is of the essence. It would be quite stupid to lose more by hanging on to falling shares than you gain in tax allowances. Better to take a big profit and pay tax than to take a smaller tax-free gain.

If you are faced with capital gains tax, consider whether you should also sell any loss makers in your portfolio. Any losses incurred in selling shares for less than you paid for them can be offset against your gains.

Again, you should not sell just for the sake of reducing your tax bill. If, after looking closely at the disappointing performer in your portfolio, you feel serious doubts about its prospects for recovery, consider selling now rather than hanging about and suffering further losses.

These arguments would also apply if you felt that a share in your portfolio was overvalued and it could be a good time to take profits voluntarily. If the sale does not push you over the capital gains limit for the year, it could be time to take a tax-free gain. Wait until the next financial year and your gains could be over the limit.

Remember the important point: sell only if you feel this is the right decision, not to artificially reduce your tax bill.

Chapter 19.
An Example Portfolio

Finally, let us look at how one investor set up a portfolio and the decisions he faced. This is a real-life (albeit simple) portfolio which we saw in the screenshot in Chapter 12. Most purchases were made in late 2009 and early 2010.

These were the reasons for investing:

- The stock market had recovered strongly from lows following the credit crunch so fears of a further collapse in share prices had receded

- The investor believed that the rally would continue and there was a serious danger of missing the best buying opportunities

- The investor had not used any of his ISA entitlement for the current financial year

- Bank accounts were paying pitifully low rates of interest well below the rate of inflation and returns on shares were likely to be more attractive.

The investor then considered what he wanted from shares. As he was retired he looked for regular dividends rather than capital growth. Because his pension put him into the higher tax bracket it made sense to invest through an ISA up to the annual allowance. He decided to invest roughly £1000 in each stock he bought to produce a wide spread of shares.

The intention was to invest the ISA allowance each tax year, either by topping up existing holdings or by investing in new companies. Once the portfolio had been built he would consider investing larger sums in each company.

The investor paid a flat £10 per trade plus 0.5% stamp duty.

Note that although this portfolio produced a steady flow of dividends, and capital gains on some stocks roughly matched losses on others over the following months, the investor did make mistakes and sometimes strayed from his game plan.

Shares bought

Date	Action	Reason
2009		
Dec 10	Bought 300 Sainsbury shares at 321p	The supermarket had recovered well under chief executive Justin King and was expected to continue to grow sales faster than rivals. We have to eat and price wars had abated, making supermarkets more attractive than most of the high street.
Dec 10	Bought 400 Barratt Developments shares at 112p	The housing sector was bombed out and since we all have to live somewhere house building was bound to pick up in the long term. This decision did not really fit the investment criteria as the dividend had been scrapped the previous year.
2010		
Jan 5	Bought 210 National Grid shares at 628p	Recommended in a newspaper with a good track record for share tipping. Solid dividend and prospects for growth in the UK and the US.
Jan 26	Bought 150 WS Atkins shares at 606p	High yield from well covered dividend. Consultancy services likely to be in demand as public and private sectors struggled with the aftermath of the credit crunch.
Jan 26	Bought 2,500 Taylor Wimpey shares at 38.75p	The shares had slowly recovered during 2009 after slumping from 440p to 6p over the previous 18 months. This purchase was wrong on two grounds. It left the portfolio heavily overweight in housebuilding and Taylor did not pay a dividend. The purchase was made in the hope of a long term capital gain which did not fit the investment criteria.

Jan 27	Bought 700 Hornby shares at 150p	Gambled on dividend being restored. Although this happened, it was a risk with two other shares in the portfolio also having failed to pay a dividend in the previous financial year.
Jan 28	Bought 60 Royal Dutch Shell at 1698p	Widening portfolio into new sector with hopes that the rising oil price would boost profits and dividends.
Jan 28	Bought 70 Johnson Matthey at 1496p	Widening portfolio into new sector. Dividend had increased over several years and was always covered well over two times by earnings.
Jan 28	Bought 400 Balfour Beatty at 268.25p	Hoping that the Government would spend on infrastructure projects to keep the economy going. However, this was yet another share that depended on construction in one form or another.
Mar 22	Bought 2,000 Speedy Hire shares at 26.5p	Rushing to use up the ISA entitlement before the financial year end. This purchase made the portfolio an even greater hostage to the fortunes of construction. It is dangerous to buy shares in haste for tax reasons.
Apr 7	Bought 500 Severfield Rowen shares at 205p	Recommended in the press; spread the portfolio into manufacturing; started to use new financial year's ISA allowance early to avoid another last minute rush; higher than average yield well covered by earnings so fitted the objects of the portfolio perfectly.
Apr 16	Bought 2,000 Speedy Hire shares at 34.25p	Fears about missing the boat after rise in share price since first purchase. The original stake was valued at only half the size of previous purchases so this put Speedy Hire on a par. However, buying in two batches doubled the dealing costs. The investor was hesitant to make a larger initial investment and the fundamentals had not improved since.

Portfolio valuation (at start)

The shares purchased resulted in a portfolio as shown in the following table.

Company name	Number of shares	Purchase price (p)	Cost (£)	Weighting (%)
WS Atkins	150	606	919.41	7.9
Balfour Beatty	400	268.25	1,087.98	9.4
Barratt Developments	900	112	1,022.54	8.8
Hornby	700	150	1,053.99	9.1
Johnson Matthey	70	1,496	1,062.27	9.1
National Grid	210	628	1,153.76	10.0
Royal Dutch Shell	60	1,698	1,034.13	8.9
Sainsbury	300	321	975.60	8.5
Severfield Rowan	500	205	1,040.13	9.0
Speedy Hire	4,000	26.5/34.25	1,232.43	10.7
Taylor Wimpey	2,500	38.75	989.56	8.6
Total			11,571.80	100

Dividends received

Despite its flaws the portfolio did bring in a stream of dividends over the next few months.

Date paid	Company	Period	Dividend	Amount received
Mar 17	Shell	Q4	26.36p	£15.81
June 9	Shell	Q1	27.37p	£16.42
July 5	Balfour Beatty	Final	7.2p	£28.80
July 16	Sainsbury	Final	10.2p	£30.60
Aug 3	Johnson Matthey	Final	27.9p	£19.53
Aug 18	National Grid	Final	24.84p	£37.26
Aug 18	Speedy Hire	Final	0.2p	£ 8
Aug 20	Hornby	Final	5.0p	£35
Sep 8	Shell	Q2	26.89p	£16.13
Sept 24	WS Atkins	Final	18.25p	£27.37
Total to end-Sept				£234.92

Issues faced

Even on this modest portfolio decisions had to be taken in the light of economic developments.

WS Atkins

Trading updates and results indicated that the company was doing well despite tough conditions, particularly in the rail division, and although results for the year to 30 June 2010 showed profits down on the previous year they were still ahead of 2007-8 and the dividend was increased. Long term public sector contracts gave good visibility of earnings. There was no reason to get out but a decision on whether to top up the holding depended on one's views of how hard the new government would try to persuade consultants to accept reduced payments.

Balfour Beatty

Turnover, profit and dividend have continued to rise so it was worth considering adding to holdings, especially as the shares settled around the purchase price and looked well supported. The big worry was whether the large infrastructure projects that Balfour depends on would be affected by cutbacks beyond the company's control.

Barratt Developments

Full year figures to June 30 showed a heavily reduced loss, but a loss nonetheless, postponing any return to the dividend list. House prices stagnated and first time buyers still had difficulty obtaining mortgages. The shares peaked at 139p and it was sensible to consider getting out as they fell below the purchase price. It is difficult to stand a loss, especially when the shares are in an ISA and cannot be set off against tax on any capital gains elsewhere, but it was sensible to consider biting the bullet and perhaps buying back in when the housing market eventually showed some signs of life.

Hornby

Anyone running a stop loss would have got out quickly as the shares fell 30% but those made of sterner stuff were rewarded with a recovery following the resumption of the dividend. One worry is whether purchases of toys and models will be ditched in favour of essential items. Hornby has outsourced manufacturing to lower cost countries and any rise in the value of the Chinese yuan would increase costs and cut margins. The lower pound has increased the cost of imports but has helped exports.

Johnson Matthey

The group has diversified into a wide range of metals but the fortunes of the motor industry have an impact on the catalyst side and should be borne in mind. Earnings and profits have held up well in the recession and, although the P/E and yield became less attractive than the market average, the share price factored in a continued rise in profits. It was therefore important to monitor trading updates for any warning signs.

National Grid

Shareholders were faced with an unwelcome decision when a rights issue came out of the blue. The shares immediately fell, giving investors no time to get out. The results accompanying the announcement were good, so it was sensible to buy the deeply discounted rights shares. Proceeds of the new issue along with strong cash flow should pay for heavy capital spending but shareholders should watch for any dent in the cash flow, which could trigger another rights issue.

Royal Dutch Shell

With the oil price creeping back up towards $100 a barrel there were few concerns about Shell and an increased quarterly dividend was welcome. The dividend is set in US dollars so changes in the exchange rate can affect the payout. Oil is found in volatile places – rebels in Nigeria have been a particular problem for Shell – so the geo-political climate should be borne in mind, as should the state of the global economy. At least Shell is not dependent on just one or two markets.

Sainsbury

Sales continued to grow but it was vital to watch the like-for-like quarterly figures of all the major supermarkets to see who was gaining ground and who was losing market share. Also important was how well Sainsbury's more expensive Taste the Difference was faring as any trading down by shoppers into basic ranges would affect margins. Ignore petrol sales as these are highly erratic and supermarkets make comparatively little profit from them.

Severfield Rowan

Shares in this highly cyclical industrial engineering stock had plummeted when the recession bit and were recovering slowly, so the market was clearly nervous. Persistent talk of a double dip recession meant shareholders should be on guard to take profits if the worst came to the worst. It was particularly important to read the outlook in each trading update. On the other hand, the further the recovery staggered on, the more secure the respectable yield looked.

Speedy Hire

Once a great growth stock, the plant and tool hire group had plummeted before levelling out at 20 to 30p. These shares were going nowhere until construction and housebuilding took off again but at least the shares looked to have found a floor. Claims that the group's markets had hit the bottom had to be read realistically alongside falling profits and a slashed dividend. Recovery depended on the private or public sector, or both, spending more on construction, which was highly doubtful so shareholders needed to keep a watch on the broader UK economy.

Taylor Wimpey

Much of the remarks about Barratt applied here but at least the group scraped back to profitability towards the end of 2009. Trading updates needed to be monitored for any signs of backsliding. Also recovery in the share price was likely to be slow and the resumption of a dividend was some way off so shareholders needed to decide whether it was worth hanging on for a long haul.

Lessons learnt

- Do not rush into share purchases

- Read all trading updates carefully and with a critical eye

- Above all, remember what it is you want from shares and stick to your game plan.

Sample portfolio spreadsheet

Even if one uses an online portfolio service or a specialised software program it can still be a good idea to keep a separate record of your portfolio transactions. A simple way to do this is using a spreadsheet program such as MS Excel. A template spreadsheet (for the portfolio featured in this chapter) can be downloaded from this book's webpage:

www.harriman-house.com/howtobuildashareportfolio

The spreadsheet has two worksheets:

Transactions: records the details of every trade

Portfolio: values the portfolio on a specific date and calculates the profit/loss on each holding.

Index

A

acquisitions. *see* takeover bids
active traders, 117, 118-119
advisory services, 230
aerospace sector, 83
airline industry, 89, 191-196
annual reports, 100
Antofagasta (case study), 31-32
art, 13, 19
artificial dips, 167
asset classes, 5-21
  art, 12, 19
  bonds, 11-12
  cash, 6-7
  collectibles, 12-13
  Exchange Traded Funds, 15-17
  funds, 13-14
  gilts, 10-11
  gold, 7-10
  property, 12-13
  shares, 5-6
auctions, 13, 19
automotive sector, 33, 83
averaging down, 172-175
  case study, 173-175

B

banks, 29, 82, 83
Barclays Equity Gilt Study 2009,
  24-25
bear market, 6, 123-124
  and new issues, 131
benchmarking, 4, 158, 160-162
beverages sector, 90
bonds, 11-12
  fees, 20
  yield, 103
book building, 134-135
bottom up strategy, 52–57
BP (case study), 196-201
British Airways (case study),
  191-196
broadcasting sector. *see* Media, the
Buffet, Warren
  on diversification, 26-28
  on Kraft vs. Cadbury, 185
bull market, 6, 123-124
bus companies, 89
buybacks, 214–216
buying. *see also* investment
  conditions

adding to existing holdings,
177-178
averaging down, 172-175
example portfolio, 240-241
rights issues, 203-213
after a takeover, 219-220
buy-to-let mortgages, 12-13

C

capital gains, 5, 115-122
income vs. growth, 37-38
new issues, 133-134
O'Higgins strategy, 118-122
takeover bids, 218
tax, 12, 116, 182, 233,
236-237
cash, 6-7
cash flow, 4, 181-182
catching falling knives, 147-149
Cattles (case study), 186-190
charges. see costs
choosing shares, 42-57, 219-220
bottom up approach, 52-57
data analysis, 59-75
top down approach, 47-52
City of London Investment Trust,
45
coins, 13
collectibles, 12-13
commission, 15, 19-20
company performance, 142-143
warning signs, 149
company reports, 100
company sectors, 41-42, 48-51
and economic cycles, 77-97

company valuation, 225
conglomerates, 42
construction sector, 77-78, 82, 83
case study, 143-147
consumer spending, 81-82, 83
copper, 31-32
costs, 229-232
commission, 15, 19-20, 39
conveyancing, 20
overseas trading, 34
spread, the, 231-232
stock broking services,
229-231
tax, 232-237
telephone brokering, 230-231
counter-cyclical companies, 89
credit rating, 207
crisis, financial, 125-128
impact on new issues, 131-132
'cum dividend', 100
cyclical companies, 77, 82-89
case study, 85-87
dividend payments, 105
economic downturn, and,
82-84
main sectors, 83
visibility of earnings, 81-82

D

data analysis, 59-75
forecasts, 57
historic, 59
price/earnings ratio, 60-63
dead cat bounce, 147, 199
Debenhams (case study), 135-137

defensive companies, 77, 89-98
case studies, 92-98
dividend payments, 105
main sectors, 90
pharmaceuticals, 92-95
tobacco companies, 95-98
visibility of earnings, 81-82
demergers, 224-228
case study, 226-228
diversification, 6, 20-21, 26-28,
178-179
arguments against, 26-27
weighting, 42-45
dividends, 38, 99-113
example portfolio, 243
final, 99-100
growth, 37, 112
interim, 99-100
non-payment of, 100, 105,
192-193
payment of, 99-101
prospecting, 107-110
quarterly, 99
reduced, 100-111
special, 214
tax, 100-101, 234
yield, and, 60, 101-107
Dogs of the Dow. see O'Higgins
strategy
drugs. see pharmaceuticals

E

earnings per share, 106
eBay, 13, 19

economic cycles, 77–81
cyclical companies, 77, 79-81,
82-89
defensive companies, 77, 89-98
investing for capital gain, 116
electricity sector, 107-108
emerging markets, 17, 29, 110
engineering sector. see industrial
and engineering sector
ethical investment, 97
Euromoney, 160-161
European markets, 34
Eurozone, 128, 169
exchange rate risk, 17
Exchange Traded Funds, 15-17
ex-dividend shares, 100, 167
execution only service, 229

F

falling prices, 141-151
averaging down, 172-175
stop loss system, 165-172
case study, 143-147
final dividends, 99-100
financial advisers, 14-15
Financial Services Compensation
Scheme, 17
flotation, 131-139
pulling a flotation, 138-139
food production, 90
forecasts, 59–60
visibility of earnings, 81–82
foreign exchange, 30
foreign stocks, 28-34
case study, 31-32

Forth Ports (case study), 220-222
FT Ordinary Share Index (FT30), 159
FTSE 100 index, 14, 159
    financial crisis, 125-128
    foreign stocks, 29-30
    as a performance benchmark, 161
FTSE 250, 159
FTSE 350, 159
FTSE All-Share, 159
FTSE Small Cap, 159
FTSE UK indices, 159
fundamental data, 59-75
funds, 13-14
future yield. *see* prospective yield

G

gambling, 89
Game Group (case study), 149-151
gapping, 165-166
gilts, 10-11, 20
GlaxoSmithKline (case study), 93-95
gold, 7-10
gold standard, 8
growth companies, 116-117
growth vs. income, 37-38, 39
guaranteed loss order. *see* stop loss system

H

healthcare sector, 77-78, 90
historic yield, 102

holidays, 88-89
Hornby (case study), 173-175
hostile takeovers, 219
household goods, 90
housing market. *see* property

I

IMI (case study), 85-87
Imperial Tobacco (case study), 97-98
income, investment for, 37-38, 99-113
    vs. growth, 37-38, 39
income tax, 232
independent financial advisers (IFAs), 15
Individual Savings Accounts (ISAs), 14, 37, 38, 233-236
    online management, 156-157
industrial and engineering sector, 83, 84-87
    case study, 85-87
inflation, 5, 7, 11, 24
inheritance tax, 6, 233
initial public offering (IPO), 133-134. *see also* flotation; new issues
institutional investors, 134, 213
insurance sector, 29, 90, 109-110
    case study, 210-212
interest rates, 6-7
    impact on yield, 104
interim dividends, 99-100
investment conditions, 123-130. *see also* buying

bull and bear markets, 123-124
during the financial crisis,
125-128
volatile markets, 124
investment trusts, 16, 130
IT sector, 52-56

J

Jarvis (case study), 148-149

K

Kraft (case study), 185

L

leisure industry, 87-89
London Stock Exchange, 41-42
loss limitation, 165-175. *see also*
falling prices
lump sum investment, 39-40
luxury goods, 82

M

maiden dividends, 105-106
management, 142-153
case study, 143-147
reports, 142-143, 145
manufacturing, 82
market correction, 127–128
media, the, 79-81, 83
case studies, 191-201
influence on share performance,
190-191, 192, 199

mining, 30, 31-32
motor industry. *see* automotive
sector

N

National Grid (case study),
207-209
new issues, 131-139
case studies, 135-139
financial crisis, and the,
131-132
pricing, 133-135, 136
vs. buybacks, 214
New Look (case study), 137-139
news reports. *see* Media, the

O

O'Higgins strategy, 118-122
oil industry, 29, 196-201
online auctions, 13, 19
online brokering, 19, 155-157, 230
open offers, 213-214
outsourcing, 90-92
overperforming shares, 162-163
overpriced market, 25-26,
184-185
overweight stock, 45, 163

P

Payment in Kind loan, 138
pharmaceuticals, 90, 92-95, 110
case study, 93-95

placing shares, 213-214
portfolio management, 3-4
    balance, 162-163, 179
    benchmarking, 158, 160-162
    micromanagement, 158, 218
    monitoring, 155-157
    online, 155-157
    software, 155
portfolio valuation, 242
pound cost averaging, 129
price/earnings ratio, 38, 60-62,
        115-116
primary shares. *see* new issues
Private Finance Initiatives (PFIs),
        91
profit warnings, 142, 149-151
progressive dividend policy, 37
property, 4, 12-13, 20
prospective yield, 102-103
Prudential (case study), 210-212
Public-Private Finance, 91
pulling a flotation, 138-139

Q

quarterly dividends, 99

R

rail companies, 89
raising capital
    placing shares, 213-214
    rights issues, 201-213
registration, shares, 101
regular investment, 40-41, 130
repurchase. *see* buybacks

rights issues, 167-168, 203-213
    case study, 207-209, 210-212
    warning signs, 204
risk, 178-179
    aversion, 4, 21
    bonds, 11
    case study, 191-196
    catching falling knives,
        147-149
    diversification, and, 178-179
    exchange rate, 17
    Exchange Traded Funds, 17
    reward, and, 103

S

Sage (case study), 52-57
savings, 6-7, 130
selling, 181-201
    in batches, 182, 184
    a proportion of shareholding,
        183-184, 201
    stop loss system, 165-172
share price
    artificial dips, 167
    averaging down, 172-175
    book building, 134-135
    buybacks, and, 215
    collapse, 147-148
    falling, 141-151
    media influence, 190-191, 192,
        194-195
    new issues, 133-134, 135
    opening and closing, 165-166
    overpriced, 184-185
    price/earnings ratio, 60-61

rights issues, 204-205

spread, the, 231-232

stop loss system, 165-172

takeover bids, 168, 217-218

vs. value, 118

share register, 101

Sharescope software, 155

short selling, 17, 199

short-term trading, 124

sovereign debt crisis, 128, 169

special dividends, 214

sporting events, 79, 89

spread, 231-232

spreading purchases, 129

spreading risk. *see* diversification

stagging, 134, 135

stake size, 41

stamp duty, 232

stamps, postage, 13

steel industry, 82

stock markets, 159

   benchmarking, 158

   crash, 169-170

   overseas, 33-34

stock broking services, 229-231

   online, 19, 155-157, 230

   telephone deals, 230-231

stop loss system, 165-172

sub-prime mortgage market, 125, 143, 144

   case study, 186–190

sum of the parts valuation, 225

support services sector, 90

suspension of dividends, 105

synergies, 217

T

takeover bids, 131, 168, 217-224

   case studies, 220-222, 223-224

   hostile, 219

tax, 100, 232-237

   capital gains, 116, 182, 236-237

   concessions, 233-236

telecoms, 29, 108-109

telephone brokering, 230-231

tobacco companies, 90, 95-98

   case study, 97-98

top down approach, 47-52

tracker funds, 21

transport, 89

travel sector, 82, 87-89, 191-196

U

underperforming shares, 162-163

underweight stock, 45, 163

unit trusts, 16

V

value investments, 117-118

visibility of earnings, 81-82

volatile markets, 125-128

VT (case study), 223-224

W

water companies, 90

weightings, 42-45, 163

Wolseley (case study), 143-147

Y

yield, 37, 59-62, 101-107
    bonds, 103
    calculation, 102-103
    fluctuation, 103-104